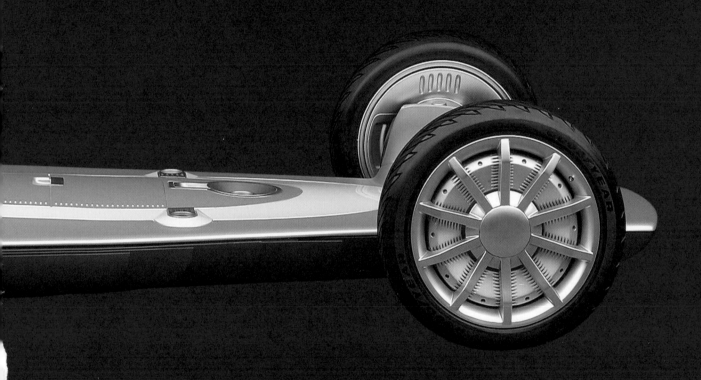

CONCEPT CARS

Larry Edsall

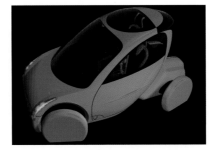
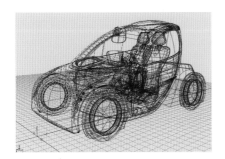
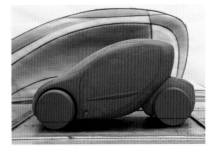

BARNES & NOBLE

NEW YORK

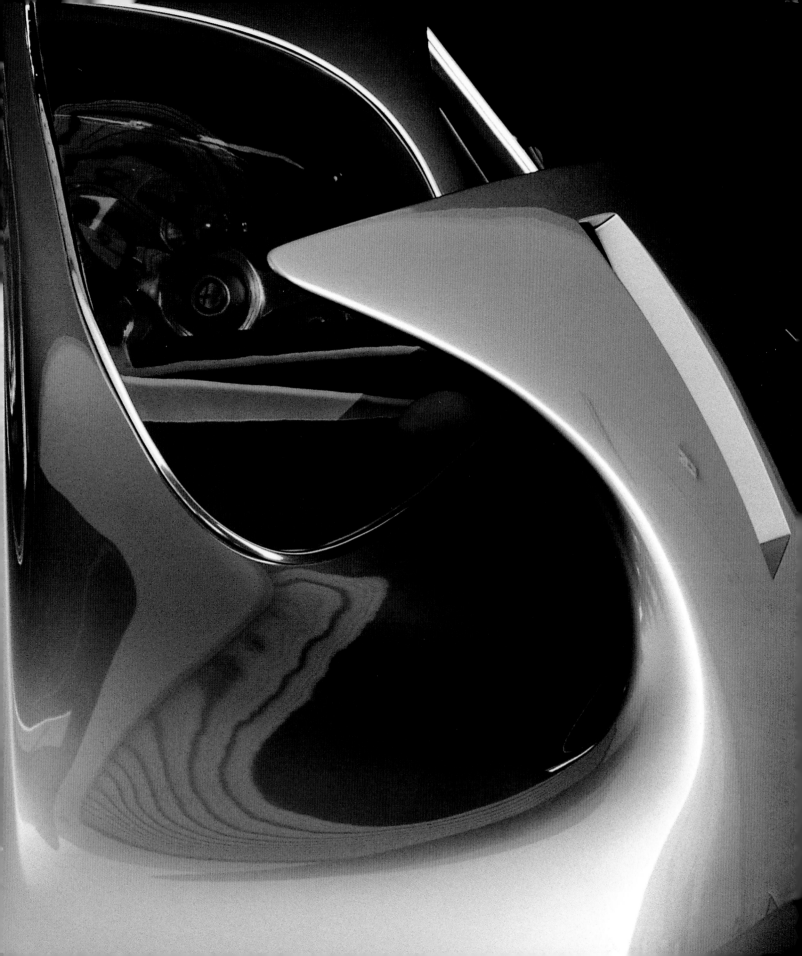

CONTENTS

TEXT

Larry Edsall

EDITORIAL PRODUCTION

Valeria Manferto De Fabianis

Laura Accomazzo - Claudia Zanera

GRAPHIC DESIGN

Maria Cucchi

---

*1 Prisma Design, a
California studio run by
former Mercedes-Benz
designer Gerhard Steinle,
designed this concept for
2030 and beyond for the
German magazine Stern.*

*2-3 With wings that are both
aerodynamic and sculptural,
BAT 5, a 1954 concept
designed by Bertone's famed
Franco Scaglione, remains
one of the most beautiful
dream cars of all time.*

*4-5 The Volkswagen
Concept 1 Cabriolet was
unveiled at Geneva in
1994, just weeks after
the hardtop version had
been the star of the
Detroit show.*

*7 At Geneva in 2001, Frank
Rinderknecht presented his
Rinspeed Advantage R^{one}
concept with a four-cylinder
engine powered by
compressed natural gas or
biofuel made from waste.*

INTRODUCTION

They are the cars we can't drive. In fact, only rarely are we even allowed to touch them. But we flock to auto shows, by the millions in the case of the major international showcases in Tokyo, Frankfurt, Geneva, Paris or Birmingham, or those staged in the large American convention centers in New York, Detroit, Chicago and Los Angeles. We go to the show just for the opportunity to see these concept cars, to see them and to dream of the day when we might actually take one for a spin around the block.

Concept cars are dream machines, vehicles that we eagerly hope will provide a forecast of our own automotive future. Here today are the cars of tomorrow. Or at least of the tomorrow as someone sees it.

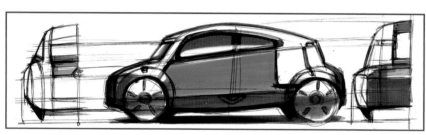

In their purest form, concept cars show us the future through the artistic eyes and creative mind of the auto designer.

"Car design is about the most complicated, creative activity I can think of," says C. Edson Armi, a professor of art history whose specialties include medieval architecture, Romanesque sculpture and the design of the modern automobile. Cathedrals and cars, that's certainly an interesting mix of academic interests.

"Designing a car involves everything from organizing people, marketing, engineering, ergonomics and, from my perspective, most impor-

tantly, aesthetics. There's fantastic nuance and a complex of activity.

"What I don't understand," Armi adds, "is why it hasn't been approached by art historians in the past. I think because it's a commercial product and art historians are too highfalutin' for that."

But even automotive historians haven't focused on concept cars and the role they play in attracting even those consumers who see their own cars as mere appliances, in infatuating the hard-core auto enthusiasts, and in inspiring entire car companies by providing a rallying point to sharpen focus in times of trouble. Desperation frequently leads to stunning concept cars. Consider the Dodge Viper, the Nissan Z or the Ford GT.

In fact, sometimes concept cars are created not to show to the public but only to inspire those inside the corporation:

"In 1989 I was vice president and I decided that all the sedans on the road were dull, drab and boring," says Chuck Jordan, who retired as vice president of design at General Motors, where he worked in the design department for more than 40 years.

"All these Japanese cars and our cars looked the same and were just appliances," Jordan continues. "There was no character. No excitement.

"I said to the guys in one advanced studio, 'hey, let's do an emotional four-door sedan, a wow car.' The guys really got into that. I said 'let's design it like Kelly Johnson used to design fighter planes in the Lockheed Skunk Works: with total freedom. Let's do it with a thin-wall body and let's pop that body out around the wheels.'

8 *Will Daeshik Kim be the next Giorgetto Giugiaro? Kim drew the sketches for an expandable car while studying at the Art Center College of Design. This concept vehicle is made of recyclable materials and has upgradable body panels that can be replaced, as a growing family needs more room.*

8-9 *The Volkswagen W12 Roadster concept was designed by Italdesign-Giugiaro and made its debut at the Geneva Motor Show in 1998. Giorgetto Giugiaro began his relationship with VW in 1969 when he was commissioned to create the Golf, successor to the famous Beetle.*

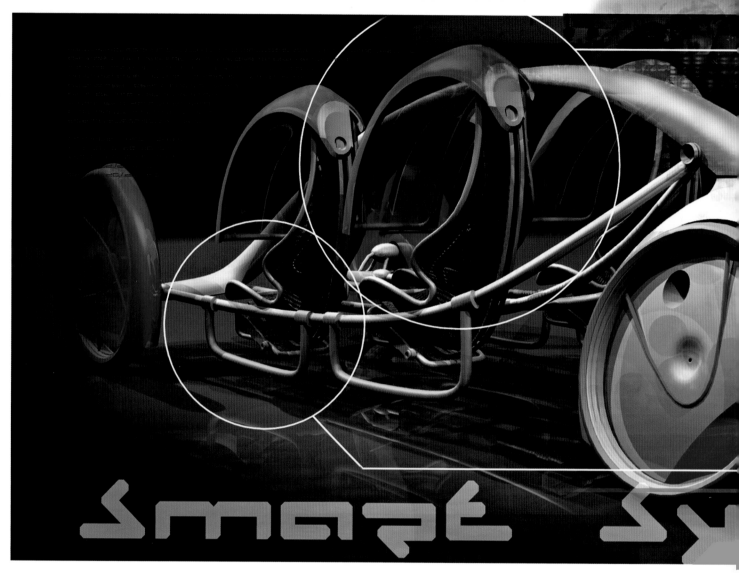

Smart Sy

"Well, we did one, from sketching to a full-size clay model and we painted it and it was double ugly.

"I said, 'no problem, let's start over.' And we did, and that one developed into a beauty and it really looked slick. It was exciting. You looked at it and said, 'Wow!'

"We made a fiberglass of that car and put it on the second floor when the General Motors management and every designer had to walk by several times a day. We put it on a carpet and under a spotlight; that was a little Harley Earl trick.

"One day the general manager of Oldsmobile came to me and said, 'we're going to drop the Toronado and we want to replace it with a sporty four-door sedan. Can we have that design that you have out in the hall?'

"That design became the Aurora."

Harley Earl had been Jordan's first boss at GM. Years earlier, he had been the creator of the first concept car. In many respects, he created the entire concept and methodology of American automotive design, and his influence spread around the globe.

AVATAR
PUBLIC TRANSPORT 2050

Earl grew up in Hollywood, where he helped his father build custom cars for movie stars.

Ever since his arrival in Detroit, concept cars have been as much about show business as about auto business, as much about sex appeal as they are about technological innovation, and in many respects new technology is the motor the drives the concepts. Concept cars, says one auto designer, are where the magic happens.

Another says that concept cars are three-dimensional question marks on wheels, question marks that ask "What if?"

Art historian Armi predicts that 100 years from now, cars will be considered great works of art. If he's right, then concept cars are the true masterpieces.

ROTATABLE WINDSHIELD FOR BETTER ACCESS.

SIDE BODY-GUARD SWINGS UP, PROTECTING PASSENGERS FROM LATERAL SHOCK.

Stem

10-11 and 11 bottom Art Center of Design student Carl Vetillard proposed an automated commuting system, appropriate for the Los Angeles area. The system comprises lightweight, hydrogen-powered and automated bicycle-style vehicles that navigate themselves from home to the place of work.

10 bottom Avatar is a public transportation concept design by John Bondoc, a student at the Art Center.

12-13 The Dodge Viper GTS Coupe concept debuted at the Los Angeles auto show in 1993 and went into production in 1996.

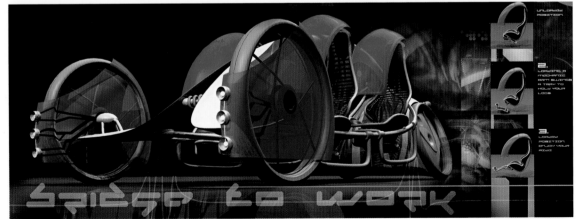

bridge to work

THE BUICK Y-JOB

I n the 1930s, it was commonplace for carmakers to use the letter "X" to identify their experimental prototypes, vehicles that most often were studies in streamlining, or as close to streamlining as anyone got in the days when cars were just beginning to become more than boxes on wheels.

Austrian mathematician Paul Jaray was among the first to experiment with streamlining. Jaray worked on dirigibles and applied his studies in an early wind tunnel to sculpt himself a unique Audi with a long and rounded nose and swept-back windshield. Battista "Pinin" Farina put a tapered, almost teardrop-shaped body on a Lancia. In the United States, Chrysler did the Trifon Special prototype that it used to develop its famed but short-lived Airflow series. Luxury automaker Pierce-Arrow produced a handful of sleek Silver Arrow cars, hoping to sell them in a desperate effort to raise enough money to keep the company in business. Cadillac used the Chicago Century of Progress world's fair to unveil its V16 Aero-Dynamic Coupe. But to be a true "dream car" a vehicle would need to go beyond experimental aerodynamics. It would have to be inspirational, combining design, technology and innovation to show the road to the future in such an exciting way that those who saw it would be eager to ride along.

Then as now, dreams were among the chief products of the Hollywood film factories, and it was from the home of motion pictures that young Harley Earl carried a dream to Detroit, the center of the automotive world. Ironically, Harley Earl's father, W.J. Earl, had moved west from Michigan, had gone to California and established Earl Automotive Works, which built custom cars for Hollywood stars. Young Harley left his studies at Stanford University to work for his father's business. Among his first

projects was the creation of custom bodywork for silent movie star Roscoe "Fatty" Arbuckle and for early cowboy movie hero Tom Mix.

Cadillac's West Coast distributor Don Lee bought Earl Automotive Works and pointed out Harley Earl's talent to Lawrence Fisher, Cadillac's general manager back in Detroit. General Motors wanted to develop a new model to fill the gap between its Buick and Cadillac lines, so Fisher and General Motors president Alfred P. Sloan Jr. recruited Harley Earl to create the styling for that new vehicle. In the early days of the horseless carriage, automobiles were little more than boxes on wheels: a box to cover the engine and various mechanical components, a bigger box to provide protection from the

The first dream car
even had a special name

14-15 The LaSalle (that's a 1929 model, with the designer at the wheel) was Harley Earl's first styling effort for General Motors.

14 bottom Before moving to Detroit to head GM's new Art and Color Section, Earl worked for his father's company, Earl Automotive Works, designing custom coachwork for cars driven by Hollywood stars.

15 top Harley J. Earl joined GM in 1926 when he was 34 years old and led its design department until just before his retirement in 1959.

15 bottom Harley Earl's first car for GM was the 1927 LaSalle, which was chosen as pace car for the 1927 Indianapolis 500. A few weeks after the race, a LaSalle averaged more than 95 miles per hour in a 10-hour endurance test at GM's Proving Grounds. The feat was remarkable considering the Duesenberg that won the 500-mile race had averaged 97.5 mph.

Those who could afford it had complete bodies created by custom coachbuilders such as the Earl Automotive Works in America or by even more famous companies in Europe, but Harley Earl's 1927 LaSalle is widely considered to be the first production car that was designed rather than merely engineered. "I have a quote on a little plaque on my desk," says Wayne Cherry, who in 1992 became only the fourth person to succeed Harley Earl as General Motor's vice president of design.

"It's from July 8, 1926 and it was Alfred Sloan talking about how vehicles were pretty much alike mechanically and had become reliable and that it was the style that was going to differentiate vehicles in the future. It was his vision to bring someone like Harley Earl in to start that."

weather for the driver and passengers, and smaller boxes attached to running boards or the back of the car to carry tools and luggage. The most popular car, the car that actually made cars popular, was Henry Ford's Model T, which was a very tall — and always black — box on wheels. Automakers, and especially custom coachbuilders, would elongate some of the boxes, particularly those over ever longer and more powerful engines, and a vehicle's appearance could be further enhanced with handsome grilles, with sculpted fenders over the wheels or by adding bright metal exhaust pipes along the vehicle's flank.

16 top Harley Earl set up GM's new Art and Color Section in 1927. The photo shows the section at work in the late 1930s. Earl thought Art and Color sounded sissified and the name changed to GM Styling in 1940, then to GM Design in 1972.

16 center Among the innovations that Harley Earl introduced to automotive styling was the clay model, done both in small scale and in full-size proportions.

16 bottom In addition to doing colored paintings of their vehicle proposals, Harley Earl's designers did orthographic projections with the vehicle's front, side and rear displayed in full-size outlines.

16-17 Harley Earl's innovations extended well beyond the design studio. International motor shows, such as this 1929 show at London's Olympia provided a somber showcase for new vehicle introductions until Earl and GM included Broadway-style entertainment in their Motorama extravaganzas.

While cross-town rival Henry Ford was building those basic black Model T and eventually his updated Model A cars, Sloan saw General Motors' future in providing style, comfort, color in an ongoing succession of new models. Impressed by Earl's work on the LaSalle, Sloan broke design away from the engineering department and in 1927 created the Art and Color Section of General Motors, with 34-year-old Harley Earl in charge of the styling of all the company's cars, a position he would hold until he retired in 1959.

Earl lived up to his Hollywood image. He was tall, flamboyant and outspoken. Some say he could barely draw. But he had a knack for knowing the public and its tastes, and for being able to inspire his design team to fulfill those automotive dreams.

"He had a sense of theater like very few before or after him," says J Mays, vice president of design for General Motors' historic rival, the Ford Motor Company. Among those who would be inspired by Earl was Chuck Jordan, who went to GM as a young designer in 1949 and worked under Earl and his successor Bill Mitchell.

"There's only one Harley Earl," says Jordan, who retired in 1992 as General Motors' fourth vice president of design. "Timing's everything," Jordan continues. "He'd never last today with all the political correctness. He was a dictator. He'd fire you on the spot. But he had an uncanny knack of knowing what to do and what the public would eat up. He was just a master of that."

Larry Faloon, another retired GM designer and the department's unofficial historian, notes that back in Hollywood, the Earls lived perhaps as close as next door to the DeMilles, as in epic moviemaker Cecil B., and Harley Earl grew up with "this built-in

sense of showmanship." Earl certainly put that showmanship to good use in his — and the world's — first true concept car, the 1938 Buick Y-Job. Because this car went beyond experimental, Earl took the car's name from the aircraft industry, which used the "Y" designation for its most advanced work. Earl's 1938 Buick Y-Job was much more than an experiment in rounding off the edges of a box on wheels, although it certainly had dramatic and aerodynamic styling. Its cut-in running boards were concealed by its long doors, which themselves had unique flush handles.

The Y-Job also had such innovative and futuristic — and previously unseen — technology as a power convertible top, electric windows, hidden headlights and many other features that decades later would be part of even ordinary production cars.

The Y-Job was built to point the way to that future, and to excite those who would see it about where the automobile could take them. But it also was built as Harley Earl's daily driver, the car he drove for many years from home to work and to the country club. Late in 2002, the Y-Job's odometer shows 25,849 original miles, including several hundred recently acquired at the Goodwood Festival of Speed in England.

"The car's never been repainted and we've never rebuilt the motor," Larry Faloon notes as he leads the way into the GM Design Center in Warren, Michigan, a northern suburb of Detroit. Down one hallway, then left along an even longer hallway and finally another left turn and Faloon opens the door to the Mechanical Assembly garage, the very garage Earl had built on the ground floor of the building for the construction and maintenance of special vehicles his staff would design.

18 top While Henry Ford was cranking out black Model Ts, GM president Alfred P. Sloan Jr. recognized the impact design and color could have on sales. Sloan is shown receiving a scroll of appreciation from GM factory workers in 1936.

18-19 and 19 top Freed from the constraints of merely laying bodywork over mechanical components, Harley Earl and his Art and Color Section designed the first dream car, the 1938 Buick Y-Job.

And there, much as it looked when Harley Earl drove it, is the Y-Job, parked just in front of the 1951 LeSabre, the Y-Job's successor both as an early and significant General Motors concept car and as Earl's daily driver. Also in the garage for some work are two other later General Motors concepts — the Chevrolet Mako Shark and the Aerovette; both are being readied to take part in the Corvette's 50th anniversary celebration taking place in 2003.

Faloon notes that with careful repair and maintenance through the years, the Y-Job remains fully operational, except for the doors that conceal its

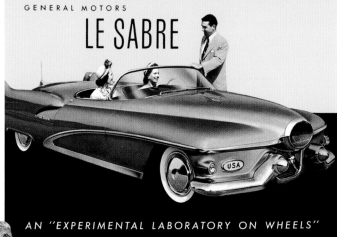

GENERAL MOTORS
LE SABRE
AN "EXPERIMENTAL LABORATORY ON WHEELS"

hidden headlights need to have new ring gears engineered. He and the car's keepers demonstrate how the top and windows still power up and down, how the concealed running boards were designed, how the dashboard was developed for ease of use long before ergonomics would become part of the automotive lexicon.

The Y-Job was built on a standard Buick Century platform and was powered by the division's 320 cubic inch, 141-horsepower inline eight-cylinder

on a magnesium bridal and specially engineered chrome molybdenum steel chassis. It was powered by a unique, 90-degree V8 engine with an aluminum block and a Roots-type supercharger, with two Bendix Eclipse side-draft carburetors that metered two fuels: methanol being used as a high-rpm knock suppressor, just as it was on World War II fighter planes. Earl and his designers were inspired by jet aircraft and the LeSabre also has an altimeter. Its speedometer is a rotating disc that shows the vehicle's speed through a small window on the dashboard. The headlights are hidden and spin themselves into place. The car's rear section is patterned after an F86 jet fighter's. Additional peacetime dividends included seats covered with the same fabric that was used in bomber pilot seats, and could be

20 bottom Like the Y-Job, the LeSabre became Harley Earl's daily drive. In this photograph Harley Earl can be seen in the driver's seat.

21 right Though introduced in 1951, the LeSabre's appeal didn't diminish over time. GM president John F. Gordon watches as Jordan's King Hussein takes the wheel while touring Detroit in 1959.

engine. But instead of the standard, upright body, Earl wanted a car that was dramatically lower. Earl's team included not only stylists but also engineers and mechanics, and they worked with Charlie Chayne, Buick's chief engineer, to modify the chassis, which was lowered three inches. Overall, the highest point on the Y-Job is some eight inches lower than on the standard 1938 Buick. To get the car as low as possible, a cupped section was cut into the floorboard just behind the accelerator pedal to provide room for the driver's right heel.

To emphasize the car's low appearance, the Y-Job rides on 13-inch wheels, some three inches smaller than the standard wheels of the time. The Y-Job introduced a new, low and wide and curved grille shape that would become a Buick characteristic. It had low but wide front fenders that taper dramatically along the sides of the V-shaped hood. "This isn't as low as it looks," Faloon explains, "but because of the way he did the drop-off of the fender, it really drove the car down visually." Long, thin chrome bars accent the sides of the front and rear fenders and enhance the car's low-slung appearance, a look further emphasized by the Y-Job's long, low boat-tail trunk lid. Despite its length of more than 17 feet, the

Y-Job seats only two people. Instead of a back seat, the power convertible top folds away behind the front seats and beneath a hard tonneau cover. "It's must have startled people at the country club when he put the top up and down," says Faloon.

Even more impressive is the convertible top mechanism for the LeSabre. "The Y-Job was a beacon of what was to come," says Faloon. "It was startling, and what he followed it with was amazing." While the occupants of the Y-Job needed to manually secure the three latches the locked the top to the windshield header, the LeSabre's top was fully automatic. It also had a rain sensor located between the front seats. Although it no longer functions, Faloon has talked to people who saw the car parked at the golf club where Earl played. They report seeing youngsters run to the swimming pool and get cups of water that they'd toss into the car, just to watch the rain sensor activate the power top. "The top would come up and the windows would come up and seal the car from the rain," Faloon says, marveling at this technological showcase on wheels.

While the Y-Job was built on a regular Buick chassis and had a standard engine, the LeSabre has an even more low-slung aluminum body that rides

22 top The LeSabre's design
drew inspiration from the
F86 jet figher. The car's
speedometer was a spinning
disc that showed velocity
through a small window.
An altimeter was among
the gauges.

22-23 Aircraft design
cues for the LeSabre
included its jet-like tail
section and air brakes.
Seats were covered in the
same heated fabric as
those on which bomber
pilots sat.

plugged into an electrical source to provide a warm surface. "Even our youngest designers come down here for their lunch hour sometimes just to look around," Faloon says. "I remember the first time I saw the Y-Job," he adds.

"It was probably in the early '70s, and I remember thinking: 'Oh, my goodness'." Faloon worked for General Motors for nearly 35 years, but he's back in the Design Center often in his unofficial role as archivist and tour guide. "I was trained as a product designer, not a car person, but it was a fabulous opportunity and after working here for a few years, the thought of going back to doing toasters and refrigerators had no appeal."

23 top The initial publicity photos for the LeSabre showed it in a pale copper color, but the actual show car wore a blue-green metallic paint. The car underwent some mechanical restoration in the 1990s but still wears its original paint.

23 center Crossed American and French flags were added to the LeSabre's tail fin when the car was taken to Paris for the international motor show there in October 1951.

eneral Motors built the first dream car, the 1938 Buick Y-Job, but Chrysler presented an entire fleet of concepts for the 1941 model year.

To help snap his designers out of the aftershock of the Airflow's failure to inspire buyers, and to lure potential customers into his dealers' showrooms, Chrysler president K.T. Keller commissioned two concept cars from Briggs, the company that built bodies for and then took control of coachmaker LeBaron.

The Thunderbolt, designed by Alex Tremulis, was built on Chrysler's Saratoga chassis, and while it was

24-25 and 24 bottom Chrysler distributed postcards that proclaimed its 1941 Thunderbolt concept as "The Car of the Future!" The car had a dramatic, almost fenderless design with pontoon-like body panels covering all but the bottom portion of its wheels.

25 bottom The Thunderbolt was one of two Chrysler design concepts unveiled in 1941. While the Thunderbolt had two seats, the dual-cowl Newport had room for six. The Newport was chosen as the first concept car to pace the Indianapolis 500.

FIFTIES

Dream cars provide the ride to the future

a large car with an aerodynamic, seemingly fenderless body, it had only two seats. But it had several push-button features, including a hard top that retracted into the car's trunk.

The Newport, designed by Ralph Roberts, was built on Chrysler's Imperial chassis and featured an aluminum body with dual-cowl architecture — separate cowls ahead of each of the car's pair of three-place bench seats — as well as a cloth convertible top.

Chrysler commissioned half a dozen of each concept and sent them around the country to stimulate sales. Among those stimulated were officials of the Indianapolis Motor Speedway, who selected the Newport as the pace car for the 500-mile race. Would be 50 years before another concept vehicle, the Dodge Viper, would again pace the world's most famous race. It would be nearly a decade after the Thunderbolt and Newport before another concept car would be shown to the public. World War II interrupted everything. Dreams, and dream cars, were put on hold in the face of the horrible realities of war. But soon after the fighting stopped, first in America and later in Europe, there was an outburst of post-war optimism. As in other post-war industries, car designers quickly returned to work, and now with new things such as jet aircraft to inspire them.

CHRYSLER'S K-310
Experimental DREAM CAR

26 top Chrysler chairman K.T. Keller said the K-310 concept, unveiled in 1952, "opens new horizons for the future." This dream car launched Chrysler's "Forward Look" design theme and styling cues that would be seen on subsequent production vehicles.

Virgil Exner had worked in Harley Earl's design studio at General Motors in the 1930s and spent the war years at Studebaker. Chrysler hired him to lead its post-war vehicle design program, and he turned to Italy's Ghia coachbuilding and design studio for help, and for concepts such as the somewhat awkward-looking 1950 Plymouth XX-500 and the absolutely gorgeous 1951 Chrysler K-310. Earl and his GM design staff also were back in action, with the 1951 LeSabre, the car that succeeded the Y-Job as Earl's daily driver, and the somewhat more conventionally styled Buick XP-300. Ford did its first concept, the X-100 in 1951.

As with other post-war activities, it would take some time for the car companies to ramp up their dream machines. But once they did, those dreams took on amazing shapes and colors.

"The 1950s were crazy days," recalls Bryon Fitzpatrick, chairman of the transportation design department at Detroit's College for Creative Studies. "GM was doing its big Motoramas, Ford was doing its atomic-powered six-wheelers and some totally bizarre things, and Chrysler was pulling off the Exner cars, beautiful Italian-inspired concept cars, some of those cars were spectacular."

26-27 Like the XX-500 concept of 1951, the K-310 was built for Chrysler in Turin, Italy by Ghia, which would help design and construct Chrysler's elegantly sculptured concept vehicles for many years.

27 right Virgil Exner worked in Harley Earl's design studio at General Motors, did industrial design with Raymond Loewy and then worked at Studebaker before being hired to lead Chrysler's styling studio.

28-29 The Chevrolet Corvette went quickly from concept car to production vehicle. The concept made its debut in January 1953 at the GM Motorama. The first production models were rolling off the assembly line before the end of June.

28 bottom Although the Corvette went into production as a roadster, it was shown at the Motorama in three versions — as a roadster (left), as a fastback sports coupe badged as the Corvair, and as a station wagon called the Nomad.

29 bottom The arrow on the front quarterpanels of the Corvette roadster shown at the Waldorf-Astoria Hotel, New York, had a downward-angled wing but the wing on the production version had an upward slant.

Also spectacular were the cars being designed in Europe, whether concept vehicles such as the Bertone-styled BATs or production vehicles such as the Pinin Farina-designed 1948 Cisitalia, a car selected for display at the Museum of Modern Art in New York City. But it was at the Motorama show staged by General Motors that the American public truly lived out its automotive dreams.

"That's when concept cars really got going," says Chuck Jordan, who joined GM as a designer fresh out of college (well, actually, he still was in college when he started working for GM) in 1949 and who retired as vice president of design in 1992.

"Harley Earl was fascinated with concepts. He got us going so hard on Motorama cars that we hardly had time to work on the production cars," Jordan recalls. "But people came to expect the excitement. There was pent up demand and they were fascinated by cars and they expected to see some of these things that *Popular Mechanics* magazine was putting on its cover. They were ripe for this sort of thing. A few of the cars actually went into production, most notable was the 1953 Corvette, but even those that didn't had a lot of influence."

The Corvette was first presented in the form of three concept vehicles — a roadster, a sports coupe and a station wagon — at GM's first Motorama show, in January 1953 in the Waldorf-Astoria Hotel in New York City. Also shown at that first Motorama were the Cadillac LeMans, Oldsmobile Starfire, Pontiac Bonneville Special, Pontiac Parisienne and Buick Wildcat I concepts.

General Motors had started doing car shows in the Waldorf's famous ballroom in the 1930s, though they were private displays for New York's financial community. GM celebrated the return to new cars after the war with a public show of production cars in the Waldorf in 1949, and the following year staged what it called its Midcentury Motorama in New York's most famous hotel. But the Motorama with its show of new cars and concepts began in earnest in 1953 and ran through 1961. The show would start in New York, then moved on to such cities as Miami, Los Angeles, San Francisco, Boston, Chicago and Dallas. The concepts also would go on separate barnstorming tours.

GENERAL MOTORS MOTORAMA

IMAGINATION IN MOTION

WALDORF-ASTORIA
OCT. 16 THRU 22

30 top left This crowd filled the sidewalk near the 49th Street entrance to the Waldorf-Astoria in January 1956 as people lined up along four blocks waiting to see the General Motors Motorama.

30 top right and 31 top right "Imagination in Motion" was the theme of the GM Motorama in 1959, when the Firebird III was the star of the show. But the Motorama's run would end with its nationwide tour in 1961.

30 bottom The photograph shows the scene inside the show at the Waldorf-Astoria in January 1956.

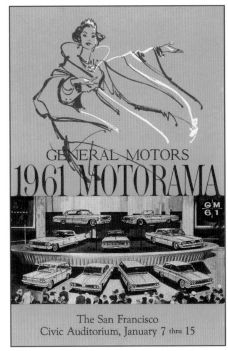

GENERAL MOTORS
1961 MOTORAMA

GM 61

The San Francisco
Civic Auditorium, January 7 thru 15

30-31 The LaSalle II
sports coupe and sedan
were the big attractions at
Motorama in 1955.

31 bottom left Among
those attending the GM
Motorama in 1953 was
the Duke of Windsor
(standing next to GM

chairman Alfred Sloan, who
sits at the wheel of the
Buick XP-300 concept car).

31 bottom right Back
across the Atlantic, the
latest designs from England
and the Continent were on
display at more traditional
auto shows.

"I can remember when I was in high school, going to a sports car race in the southern part of Indiana, and during the lunch break this big General Motors transporter unloaded the Firebird I and [three-time Indianapolis 500 winner] Mauri Rose was in there," says Wayne Cherry, a GM designer since 1962 and only the fifth person to head its design department.

"Man!" Cherry exclaims, "It was like a jet aircraft without wings. Wow!"

Just as the BAT cars would become symbols of Europe's aerodynamic oriented concept cars of the 1950s, so the trio of GM Firebirds would represent the aerospace and technological orientation of the heyday of American concepts.

Just like jet aircraft, gas turbine engines powered the Firebirds. Firebird I debuted at the 1954

Further Proof that in Styling — in Engineering — GENERAL MOTORS Leads the Way

Motorama and looked like a jet fighter with its wings clipped. It would have looked right at home on the runways of a military airport, but it looked like nothing that you might see on city streets or country highways, even though GM noted that its turbine engine powered a 110-volt generator that could provide electrical power for a household.

Firebird I had room for two people, who sat next to each other, both positioned to operate the vehicle's aircraft-style control yoke: push forward to move ahead, left or right to turn, and pull back to stop. Firebird II, introduced in 1956, supposedly was the family car of the future and had seating for four, automotive-style driving controls, pneumatic suspension, four-wheel disc brakes and such features as power windows and air conditioning. It also had a titanium body and an electric guidance system so it could drive itself along what were to be tomorrow's automated highways.

Firebird III was built for the 1959 Motorama, had a unique chassis with a central spine, a fiberglass body with Plexiglas cockpits over each of its two seats and a central stick controller (as well as automatic pilot for use on automated roads). It also had many wings, with a rear dorsal fin that was designed with only one thing in mind: It had to be tall enough to be seen above the heads of the crowd gathered around its stand in the Waldorf.

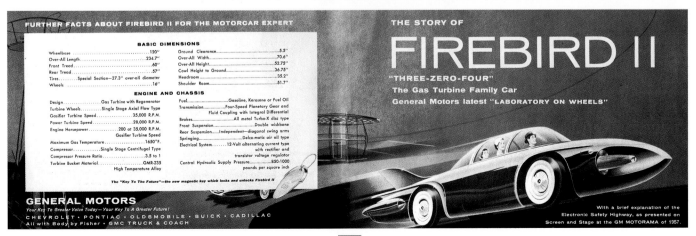

Norm James had gone to the Motorama and saw Firebird I when he was a college student, studying at design at New York's Pratt Institute. James was a young designer at GM when he and Stefan Habsburg were assigned to do the styling and technical details of Firebird III. But instead of the usual, closely scripted instructions from Harley Earl, James recalls the GM design director was nearing his retirement and provided only a basic design philosophy. Earl wanted a car similar to the 1956 Pontiac Club de Mer concept, but with a gas turbine powerplant like the other Firebirds, and there was one other thing: Earl knew that when crowds gathered

34 top Among the concepts featured at 1956 GM Motorama were the Oldsmobile Golden Rocket, which had small fins just behind the doors, (background) and the long, low-slung and shark-shaped Pontiac Club de Mer, which had separate windshields ahead of the driver and passenger (foreground).

34 bottom and 35 bottom left In the mid-1950s students at the Pratt Institute in New York explore various techniques of projecting a vehicle's design and learn to sculpt a clay scale model.

to see the cars, those standing in front blocked the view of those behind, even when the cars were elevated on display stands.

"He wanted to hold people longer," James says. "He wanted people to stick around. He wanted real entertainment value. Make them want to stay," he said, and he suggested that "when you go to Las Vegas for a stage show, you don't expect to see your wife on the stage, you expect to see a real floozy."

James recalled the dorsal wing on the Firebird I, and had just been to an air show where he saw the Nike surface-to-air missile on a steeply angled launching rack. Encouraged by Earl's comments, James abandoned the Club de Mer's "potato" shape and developed the sleek and crisp lines of the Firebird III, which appears to be sprouting wings, including a rear wing that stands nearly 60 inches tall, tall enough to be seen above the crowd at Motorama.

But to get those wings right, James had to develop a new method of car design, one that replaced velum on a vertical board and sketching. What James developed was a system that used push pins and colored yarns to trace out the vehicle's lines. He could move the pins to change those lines without leaving the distracting residue of erasure marks.

It took many moves of the pins, an initial full-size model that showed the car's lack of proportion, as well as Earl's support in the face of opposition from the official GM design committee and finally some inventive technology manipulation by Habsburg and some last-minute design tweaks by James before

"the proportions magically balanced." The process had consumed a year and a half.

James is particularly proud of what he calls the "negative space," the space you don't see, the area beneath the vehicle, which, he notes, is part of the design and can be a "very dominating space," as it is when it's the area beneath a jet fighter as it taxis down the runway. James was 26 years old when he designed Firebird III, and recalls fellow GM designer Bill Porter's comment that, "It's not the kind of car you'd take to get a quart of milk at the grocery." Earl

wanted it to be something astronauts might take to go to the rocket ship on their way to the moon.

"Ironically," James, adds, "what they actually took looked more like a milk truck."

In fact, James was involved in the design of the vehicle the astronauts drove after they reached the moon. He went from General Motors to Lockheed, where he did interior design of passenger aircraft, then was involved in the design of the lunar rover (his is one of three names holding the patent for the herringbone pattern on that vehicle's wheels).

35 top Norm James was a student at Pratt when he saw the Firebird I at the Motorama in 1954. James soon went to work for GM and helped design the tall-finned Firebird III.

35 bottom right Though staged in the mid-1950s, "People, Products and Progress, 1975" was the name of an exhibition that projected 20 years into the future. Among the designs on display was this atomic-powered automobile that featured an "automatic brain" which would assist the driver.

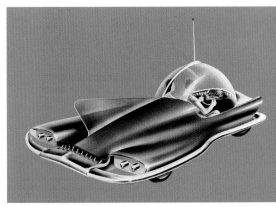

36 top and 36 bottom "Imagination in Motion" was the theme for the GM Motorama in 1959, when GM produced a brochure with images of a vehicle it proclaimed as "not just a car of the future but an automotive laboratory of today!"

36-37 A tall dorsal fin made Firebird III stand out in the crowd. Earl wanted the rear wing tall enough so it could be seen over the heads of the people crowded around its stand at the Motorama show. He knew people wouldn't leave until they'd moved close enough for a personal look.

Porter, now retired from GM but still teaching design history to automotive design students, recalls that he was just starting his career at General Motors when the Firebird III as being completed. He remembers it as "the all-time American show car," but adds that this astonishing car signaled the "end of that great show car era. I remember thinking that so much of it was cornball, so silly, even though I was drawing it just like everyone else. But in retrospect, it was a wonderfully exuberant era.

In retrospect, James compares Firebird III to a mermaid and to a downhill ski racer. "A mermaid really is totally wrong," he says, "but it isn't all that bad."

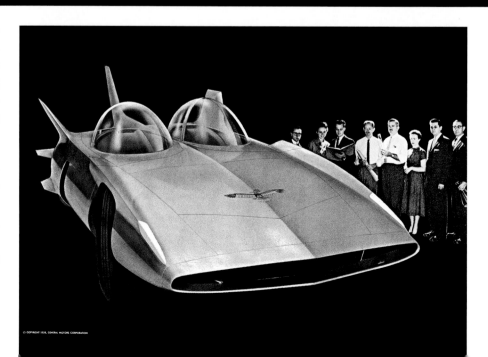

In skiing, "The guy who wins the race is not graceful, but is literally on the verge of disaster. In design, the closer you can come to doing the forbidden things, without going over the edge, the more exciting it's going to be, and the car really did get a lot of attention.

"But," he adds, "after Firebird III, wings started disappearing. We'd taken them to an extreme."

Despite Exner's elegantly designed, Italian-built concepts for Chrysler, vehicles such as the strangely shaped Ghia Selenes and Pininfarina X, the General Motors' Firebirds and Ford's bizarre X-

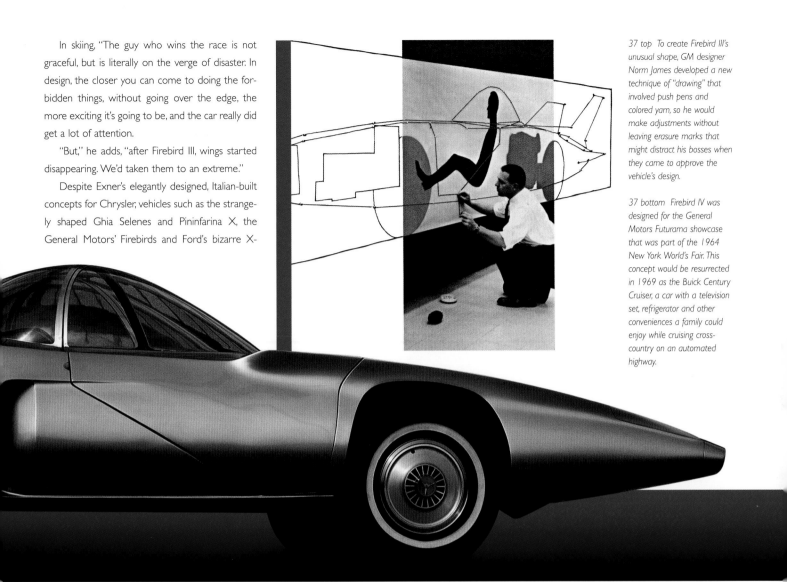

1000, its hovering Volante, its self-balancing and two-wheeled Gyron and especially its "nuclear-powered" Nucleon had taken concept cars to an extreme.

The immediate post-war years were the heyday for concept cars that reflected the same sort of extreme optimism and eagerness for the future that made Walt Disney's Tomorrowland such a popular place. Very soon, today would present challenges that became much more important than tomorrow's dreams.

Harley Earl's retirement marked the end of an era. Just ahead were new realities that would divert the designers' energies and would change the shape and scope of their dream machines.

"EX" MARKS THE SPOT

But why is it in Italy?

General Motors wasn't the only American automobile manufacturer that was building spectacular concept cars in the 1950s.

Virgil Exner and the Chrysler design department produced such stunning concepts as the K-310, the Thomas Special, the D'Elegance, the DeSoto Adventurers and Dodge Firearrows and Dart. Well, at least they did the designs, but the actual cars were built not in Detroit, U.S.A., but in Turin, Italy.

And "Ex" wasn't alone in turning to Turin for concept construction and design guidance. In the years before and after, automakers from around the world would make their own pilgrimages to the city many people know only as the home to the Holy Shroud and the 2006 Olympic Winter Games.

But how has this city become so important to concept cars and their construction? Why has Italy, the relatively small nation that dips its boot into the blue waters of the Mediterranean Sea, exerted so much influence over more than a century of automotive design?

Paolo Caccamo answers that question with one of his own. Caccamo is not a car designer. But he is an engineer who has worked for decades with many of Italy's best designers.

"Why was it in the Renaissance period that the majority of painters, sculptors and people from the arts were from Italy?" asks Caccamo, the chief exec-

utive officer of the I.DE.A. Institute, which has become one of the city's more important automotive design and engineering firms. "Or," Caccamo wonders, laughing as speaks the suggestion, "you could answer that it's because we eat so much spaghetti. I don't know whether there is a reason. It just is so." "It is, says Caccamo, something in the very nature of the Italian character that "makes us individualists and, in particular, creative. It is something that is in the nature of the Italian life, of the way we are and the way we live."

The automobile has been part of the way people in Turin are and live since 1899, when Giovanni

Agnelli established the Societa Anonimo Fabbrica Italiana di Automobili Torino and had Aristide Faccioli design the first FIAT, a vehicle with a rear-mounted, two-cylinder engine that produced four and a half horsepower and carried the vehicle and its occupants to speeds as fast as 35 miles per hour. Turin grew to become Italy's center of automotive manufacturing. Vincenzo Lancia left Fiat and established his own auto company, and there have been others, as well as dozens of coachbuilders, shops of varying size that crafted special bodies and fittings for those early automobiles and established the city's tradition of craftsmanship and advanced engineering.

Some of those garages grew to do full-scale production. Some evolved into automotive design houses. Some would emerge among the world's leaders in design as well as advanced engineering, production and technology.

In Turin a concept car could go from its first sketch through the various and detailed stages of develop-ment and construction to a finished vehicle for the show stand, or even for production.

"Centered in Torino, Italy, there is a concentration of designers and technology," notes native son Sergio Pininfarina, who adds that Turin became "sort of an Italian Detroit, the center of the automobile. But Torino had something more," he adds.

39 bottom right Battista Pininfarina visits the Alfa Romeo factory at Arese to inspect the production of one of his company's designs.

40 top In 1934, Harley Earl of General Motors toured Europe and met Battista Farina, who designed several special bodies for Cadillac chassis. In 1949, Pinin Farina sketched a sleek, five-seat Cadillac sedan proposal.

40-41 In 1953, Pinin Farina designed a pair of concept cars for Lancia using the mechanical components from that company's rather mundane Aurelia sedan. One concept, the PF 2000, was an aerodynamic coupe with a long rear greenhouse area. The other was this handsome roadster, designated as the PF 200. Among the notable design cues shared by the Lancia concepts is a large, round and distinctive front air intake.

41 top The 1954 Cadillac Cabriolet Speciale was a Pinin Farina concept for a long, streamlined two-seater with the Cadillac "V" placed high inside a distinctive round grille.

42-43 Pinin Farina's design for the Cisitalia 202 is considered to be one of the most important and artistically pleasing works in the history of the automobile. The Cisitalia featured a low hood, a wide grille and

established a look that would be copied by other post-war vehicles. The car's design was so significant that the Cisitalia was the first car selected for permanent display at the Museum of Modern Art in New York City.

"There were men like Bertone, and like my father. It was a city of production, production, production, but also of creation."

Two fathers of Turin's automotive design community were Guiseppe Bertone, who established his coachbuilding business in 1912, and was followed by his son Nuccio, and Pininfarina's father, Battista "Pinin" Farina, whose older brother started a coachbuilding business in 1906. Battista worked for his brother, then started his own company after World War I. Battista was the youngest of nine children and was called "Pinin," or "youngest" by his family. In 1961 his nickname became formally attached to his family's name. His son, Sergio, introduced him to Enzo Ferrari and together they designed and produced many of the world's most famous sports cars.

Early in his career at General Motors, Harley Earl toured Europe with his new LaSalle model and among

the people he met was Battista Farina. In 1931, Earl hired Farina to create the bodywork for a special Cadillac, the V16 Spider "Bateau," for the Maharajah of Orchha. Immediately after World War II, Pininfarina was doing design sketches for possible Cadillac models and in the 1950s built the Cadillac Cabriolet Speciale, Cabriolet 4-Posti, the Starlight Coupe and in 1961 the famed Brougham "Jacqueline."

pininfarina

During this same period, Bertone also was doing concepts for companies ranging from Fiat to Ford to Ferrari. Through the years, many of Turin's leading auto designers would become attached to the extended Pininfarina or Bertone families.

For example, Lorenzo Fioravanti worked at Pininfarina before he joined Ferrari and then launched his own design house. Giorgio Giugiaro, son and grandson of fresco painters, went to Fiat as a teenage apprentice in the design department went on to become the lead designer at Bertone and then at Ghia before he and associates founded Italdesign. When Giugiaro left Bertone, he was succeeded by Marcello Gandini.

Fioravanti, Giugiaro and Gandini would have many "brothers," people such as Ercole Spada, Pietro Frua, Franco Scaglione and so many more.

It was Scaglione who had preceded Giugiaro as design director at Bertone, where he designed what are considered to be among Italy's first true dream cars, the BATmobiles. BAT was the abbreviation of Berlinetta Aero-dinamica Tecnica, although it proved ironically fitting that bat also was the English name of the mysterious flying mammal.

Bertone's website notes that "the acronym was a great hit in the English-speaking world because the car was actually reminiscent of a bat, with its tail shape hinting at two tucked-in wings."

There were three BAT aerodynamic concept cars, all built over the chassis of the 1952 Abarth 1400 coupe with 100-horsepower powertrain mechanicals borrowed from the Alfa 1900 Sprint. BAT 5 debuted in 1953, BAT 7 in 1954 and BAT 9 in 1955.

BAT 5 was a study in high-speed stability.

Scaglione's body featured bullet-shaped front fenders, covered wheels, a raked windshield that blended into an almost flat roof, side windows canted inward at 45 degrees and a long, split rear window between two fins that flowed upward and inward. The car was a success both in aerodynamics and aesthetics.

A year later, BAT 7 took those same styling cues but took them to an extreme with much taller fins.

BAT 9 was somewhat more conservatively styled, with the wheels exposed and with smaller, more vertical planes instead of large, curving bat wings. However, there were now smaller, horizontal wings running through the middle of the car's doors and rear fenders.

Roberto Piatti, who manages the design division of Bertone, notes that after World War II, while British designers stayed with tradition and the Americans went to excesses with wings and chrome, "with Italian cars the expression of speed and power was delicately linked to the formal ele-

gance of exterior features."

For many years the Pininfarina-designed 1947 Cisitalia 202 was the only automobile exhibited at the Museum of Modern Art in New York.

Italian designers, Piatti says, could draw on the heritage of the coachbuilding era, a Renaissance period of "finery and expressive intensity" in which customers needed cars that were an integral part of their daily lives, but at the same time they wanted those cars to be personal objects of pleasure. Meeting such seemingly dichotomous goals provided Turin's designers with a strong foundation for their work with automakers from around the world.

46 top and 46-47
In 1954, Bertone's Franco Scaglione designed the Alfa Romeo 2000 Sportiva, a concept intended for use in motorsports competition. With the sleek lines of the aluminum body, the Sportiva's 138-horsepower, four-cylinder engine could propel the prototype to speeds of 200 kilometers per hour, or nearly one mile per hour per horsepower.

47 top In addition to a pair of Sportiva coupes, two spider prototypes were produced. Both versions showed influences of the BAT 5 concept car that Bertone had unveiled the previous year, especially in the way that Scaglione evolved the concept's dramatic rear wings into a more practical application on the Sportiva.

A LOST DECADE?

Bertone's exotic BATmobiles and Chrysler's sleek Ghia-built concepts were just the beginning of the post-war automotive recovery by Italy and its Turin-based concept car creators, who would dominate dream car design in the 1960s (if not well beyond) with their frequently exotic shapes. And the Italians were not alone. Design studios and automotive engineers in Germany, Britain, Sweden, France and elsewhere in Europe were exploring concepts that addressed everything from speed to safety to shapes that might reduce fuel consumption.

48 top and bottom The E2A (drawing and racing version) was the prototype for the Jaguar XK-E, which made its debut at the Geneva Motor Show in 1961. The E-type is considered among the world's all-time classic automotive designs.

48-49 Ferdinand Alexander "Butzi" Porsche works in 1961 on a clay model for a new vehicle from the company that bears his father's name. The new car, powered by a six-cylinder engine, is introduced late in 1964 as the Porsche 911.

Only in America

50-51 The XJ13 was the car that Jaguar thought might carry it back to glory in the 24 Hours of Le Mans race. However, only one original prototype was built in 1966 and the program was halted almost immediately by the merger of Jaguar and BMC into British Motor Holdings. A new 5-liter V12 engine propelled the prototype to a top speed of around 175 miles per hour on a British test track.

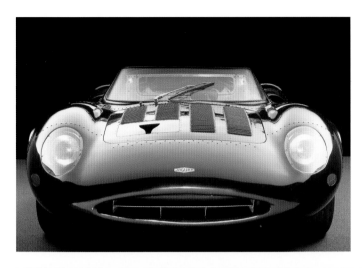
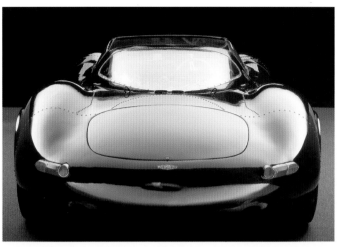

52-53 Pininfarina's 1969 design for the Ferrari 512S "Speciale" concept used a minimal amount of glass. The concept was built around Ferrari's famed 512S endurance racecar that competed in the 24 Hours of Le Mans and other events.

Because of its underpinnings, the concept had its steering wheel on the right-hand side. It also had a 550-horsepower V12 engine. While the Ferrari 512S "Speciale" was wide — some 77 inches — it also was extremely low — not quite a meter at its highest point.

53 top The Sigma Grand Prix monoposto F1 was designed as a state-of-the-art racecar in 1969 by Pininfarina, which worked with the Swiss magazine Revue Automobile and other companies. Their goal was to reduce the risk inherent in racing. The car's body was

designed so that its wheels would not interlock with those of another "open-wheel" race. The Sigma GP had a special fuel tank, an automatic fire-fighting system for the driver and engine compartments, as well as seven-point safety harness and other features.

54-55 Dino was the name of Enzo Ferrari's late son, so only a very special vehicle could carry his name. That vehicle was the Pininfarina-designed Ferrari Dino, introduced in the form of the Dino Berlinetta Speciale at the 1965 Paris show. The car, powered by a V6 engine mounted behind the seats, went into production in 1967. Sergio Pininfarina calls the Dino a "milestone" in automotive design. "That car was the 'mother' of so many Pininfarina and Ferrari cars," he says, "and also the 'mother' of many designs by my competitors."

56 top and center Astro I was a General Motors concept for 1967. It had no doors. The roof panel pivoted up and out of the way. Power "elevator" seats eased entry and exit from a car less than 36 inches tall.

56 bottom The Chrysler Turboflite was a 1961 concept with a glass canopy top that automatically lifted when either of the vehicle's doors was opened.

56-57 Astro III has two front wheels mounted next to each other. Rear wheels are housed in pods connected to the aircraft-shaped fuselage by wing-like panels.

57 top Astro II was a 1967 General Motors concept used to test mid-ship placement of a V8 engine. The sleek body, which had no headlights, was added for the auto show circuit.

Meanwhile, in America, "most designers consider the '70s a lost decade," says Bill Porter, who designed cars for General Motors from 1958 until his retirement in 1996 and who teaches college-level classes in the history of design.

In 1965, Ralph Nader published his book, *Unsafe at Any Speed*. A year later the American government, which had just issued rules mandating that new cars be equipped with seat belts, passed legislation that established a long list of additional safety standards. Then, in 1970, the first Earth Day observation spurred passage of clean air regulations.

In 1973, the oil embargo and long lines at gas pumps led to the passage of additional federal automotive standards, this time concerning fuel economy. And there was be another such oil crisis, this one in 1979 after the overthrow of the Shah of Iran. "People do not understand the

enormous drain of intellectual power that it took to shrink the cars, to improve fuel economies, to make cars safer," says Larry Faloon, who joined the General Motors design staff in the mid-1960s. "It had a dramatic effect, even on designers."

"The spirit went out of it," Bill Porter remembers. But while the American designers were suffering, the Europeans — especially the Italian design houses — were producing concepts that generated strong emotional excitement, frequently with long, low and wide, wedge-shaped bodies with sharply creased surfaces and gull-wing doors. Several of their cars were presented in behalf of the American automakers, whose own designers were preoccupied. The Italian designers also were doing styling work for the budding Japanese auto industry, which sought appeal for the compact and fuel-efficient vehicles it was beginning to export.

Ghia, Bertone and Pininfarina were in their prime, and in 1968 Georgio Giugiaro, formerly the lead designer at Bertone and then at Ghia, launched his own studio, Italdesign, with former Fiat engineer Aldo Mantovani.

At first, Italdesign focused on design work for Japanese automakers, but Giugiaro also showed concepts virtually from the start under his own label, beginning at Turin in 1968 with the Chevrolet-powered Bizzarrini Manta and a year later with the Alfa-based Iguana. (Later in 1969 Giugiaro was selected by Volkswagen to design the Golf, which while a production vehicle instead of a concept stands as a breakthrough design.) Italdesign concepts for the 1970s included the Porsche-based Tapiro; the Volkswagen Karmann Cheetah; the Alfa Alfasud Caimano and New York Taxi, Maserati Boomerang, Coupe 2+2 and Medici I and II; Audi Karmann Picche; Hyundai Pony Coupe; Lancia Megamamma and Medusa; Isuzu Fiori and the BMW Karmann Quadri and the BMW M1, a limited-production car that looked like a concept vehicle, as did the DeLorean DMC 12 of the early 1980s, when Giugiaro again turned heads with Capsula, which had its mechanical components in a low-slung chassis that could be capped with a variety of bodies (a similar design philosophy would be considered revolutionary two decades later when General Motors unveiled its AUTOnomy concept).

59 top The Abarth 1600
was an Italdesign concept in
1969. The car was a two-
seater with its four-cylinder
engine mounted behind the
passenger compartment.

59 center and bottom The
Volkswagen Cheetah was a
1971 concept project by
Italdesign and Karmann. The
car had two trunks, one in
front and another behind
the vehicle's seats, just in
front of the four-cylinder
engine.

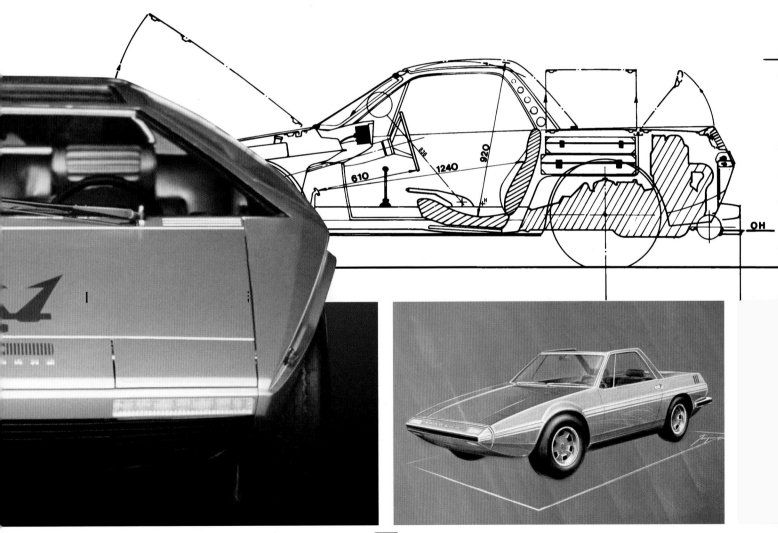

Meanwhile, Bertone had done the stunning Lancia Stratos and Siblio, Citroën Camargue, Audi Trapeze, Lamborghini Bravo, angularly shaped Alfa Navajo and Ferrari Rainbow. Pininfarina's concepts for the 1970s ranged from the spaceship-like Modulo to such aerodynamic studies as the CR25 and the CNR to concepts such as the four-door Ferrari Pinin, the boxy-shaped and electric-powered Fiat Ecos and the NSU RO 80, an upright, four-door with a retractable top.

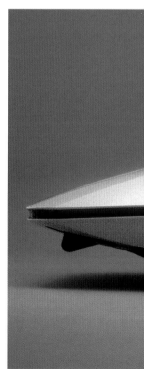

60 top and 61 bottom
Pininfarinia's Ferrari-based
Modulo won nearly two dozen
design awards after its
introduction at the Geneva
Motor show in 1970. Like the
Ferrari 512S "Speciale" from
the previous year, Modulo is
based on the mechanical
components from the Ferrari
512 racecar, although its body
is like nothing seen before,
unless it was something from
a science fiction movie.

60 bottom left and right
Modulo's body panels are
formed over a wooden buck.
The body comprises upper
and lower shells. The front of
the top shell slides forward to
provide access to the car's
passenger compartment.

61 top The 550-horsepower
Ferrari V12 engine is
mounted at the rear of the
chassis in a vehicle that
stands barely 36 inches (935
millimeters) in height.

Volvo, Renault and Mercedes-Benz presented the advances their engineers were making in automotive safety research and development in the form of concept cars. Fiat, Renault, Peugeot, Volvo and Volkswagen were among those doing concepts that showcased proposals for and actual improvements in fuel economy technology. Porsche even did a concept based on the premise that extending a vehicle's useful life on the road — by reducing internal friction, using corrosive-resistant steel and recyclable aluminum — would conserve the amount of energy consumed as vehicles were scrapped.

But the primary purpose of the European concepts cars of the era was to use aerodynamics to cheat the wind, providing the potential for extreme

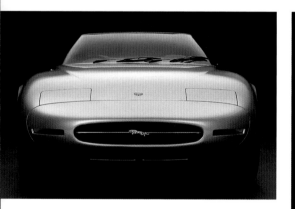

high speeds while reducing fuel use at somewhat more realistic rates of travel. Mercedes-Benz established speed records with its C111 concepts that explored both a variety of powertrains as well as aerodynamic devices to achieve speeds in excess of 250 miles per hour on an oval track.

In France, Matra made its name in motorsports, where it was extremely successful in Formula One racing. But the company begun in 1964 also was producing a succession of concept cars, many that it dis-

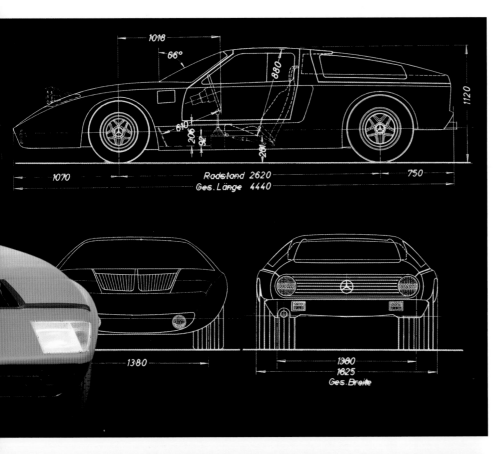

played under its own banner as well as others that bore the names of major automakers such as Renault.

"Maybe the U.S. requirements for safety were tougher than in Europe," says Jean-Louis Caussin, who began his career at Matra as a racing engineer in 1968, then for 12 years was technical director and oversaw styling before becoming executive vice president in 1994. Caussin notes that even in the 1970s, Matra was integrating the latest European regulations for safety and ecology into its concepts. Matra unveiled its M580 concept for a fuel-sipping city car in 1975, and in the years that followed rolled out a suc-

cession of interesting if unorthodox concepts, including the Rancho sport utility (which went into production in 1977), the golf cart-looking P28, the racy P29 and, to celebrate its 25th anniversary in 1989, the M25, a very small, very lightweight but very fast sports car. Matra's minivan concepts in the late 1970s led to the development and production of the Renault Espace and that company's subsequent people-mover vehicles.

62 left and 62-63 bottom Pininfarina designed this Jaguar XJS Spider concept in 1978. The design took advantage of many lessons Pininfarina had learned in the wind tunnel it built earlier in the decade. Pininfarina used its wind tunnel not only for high-speed aerodynamics, but to study how vehicle shapes could enhance fuel economy.

While its seemingly bumperless shape might save fuel, the Jaguar XJS Spider nonetheless showed elegance in its exterior styling. The car had a targa-style top that could be removed. Inside the passenger compartment, the new emphasis on safety led to a design that eliminated switchgear that might injure or distract.

Back in the United States, concept cars were pretty much put on hold while the car companies struggled with new government regulations.

"We were used to Harley Earl's philosophy," says Chuck Jordan, who joined the General Motors design department in 1949 and retired as its leader in 1992. He recalls that Harley Earl's design philosophy had been "lower, longer, wider."

"All of a sudden it was shorter, taller and narrower. It was totally opposite and we didn't know how to handle it. It took us a while to figure out how to get some emotion into a car that followed that philosophy."

Jordan admits that American concept design suffered through a "dry spell." However, that drought didn't last too long.

64 top and 65 top The 4-Rotor Corvette was designed to carry a four-rotor Wankel engine. Although GM didn't proceed with its rotary program, this gull-winged concept re-emerged in 1977 as the AeroVette powered by a conventional but powerful V8 engine.

64 bottom and 65 bottom The body for the 2-Rotor Corvette concept was created for GM in Italy by Pininfarina. Although labeled as a Corvette, this concept was designed as a possible economy-priced sports car.

65 center Like several other automakers in the 1970s, General Motors explored use of the Wankel rotary engine, which it showcased in a pair of Corvette concepts unveiled at the Paris show in 1973.

A DECADE OF

66 top and 67 bottom Ford's Dearborn, Michigan studio designed the Probe I, a concept unveiled at the Frankfurt show in 1979. The car's aerodynamic shape was designed to enhance fuel economy and visual appeal.

66 center left Even after Dearborn resumed concept car projects, Ghia continued to design Ford dream cars, including the Ghia Barchetta, which provided inspiration for the Capri roadster built in Australia.

66 center right and bottom Probe I was the first of several concepts that Ford used to explore more aerodynamic body styling. Among the others were Probe IV (center right) and Probe V (shown above in front and rear).

66-67 Probe III may look like a forerunner to the Sierra XR4i production car, but the concept included an underbody ground-effects system that lowered to enhance aerodynamic performance at speeds of more than 25 miles per hour.

he 1970s may have been the lost decade for American concept cars, but Europe was seeing everything from the exploration of body shapes and surfaces — sometimes curvy, sometimes angular — by Giugiaro, Pininfarina and Bertone to Mercedes-Benz's experimental C111 concept series and from a variety of compact city vehicles to cars that looked too exotic to be bearing British badges. Ford stayed in the concept car game by buying the Ghia studio

in 1973. Finally, in 1979, Ford's own design department, under the leadership of Don Kopka, launched the first in a series of five Probe concepts.

Probe I was introduced at the Frankfurt show and was presented as Ford's idea for a family car for the new decade. Probe I featured an aerodynamic body, on-board entertainment systems and, said Ford, could average 39 miles per gallon.

Probe II (1980) was a compact sedan. Probe III (1981) was a precursor to Ford of Europe's Sierra model. Probe IV (1983) and V (1985) were studies in extreme aerodynamics and their effect on

fuel economy. At the same time, the Japanese were starting to show some exotic concept vehicles, which often were designed with the help from Turin (consider the Honda HP-X by Pininfarina or the Mazda MX81 by Bertone).

However, by the middle part of the decade, the Japanese were displaying their own design abilities. Nissan's MID-4 was a Ferrari-like sports car and its S-Cargo took both its look and name from the shell of a snail.

About this same time, Toyota unveiled its gull-winged AXV-II sports coupe and 4500GT concept.

DELIGHTS IN EUROPE
And Detroit returns from the detour

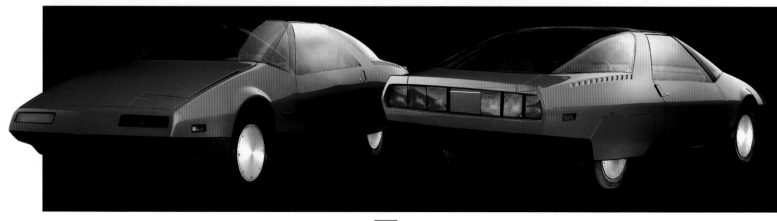

Turin's designers also were doing concepts under their own banners, or for Europe's major manufacturers. For example, in the decade of the 1980s, Pininfarina did concepts for Alfa Romeo, Audi, Lancia and Peugeot. It also maintained its own relationship with Ferrari, opening the decade with the Pinin and ending it with the Mythos.

The Pinin marked Pininfarina's 50th anniversary and was a concept for a four-door sedan, should Ferrari ever decide to build such a vehicle. The Mythos put the powertrain from the Testarossa beneath the long, low and curved body of a two-seat barchetta.

Bertone began the decade with its Athlon, a wedge-shaped, roofless speedster and in the ensuing years moved to much more geometric shapes with the Alfa-based Delfino, Corvette-based Ramarro, Citroën-based Zabrus and then showed a minivan with attitude, the Genesis powered by a Lamborghini V12.

Italdesign's concepts in the 1980s set standards for their geometric shapes and radical approaches.

The Capsula was an oddly shaped minivan, but it was more than that because it featured a low-slung chassis on which could be placed a variety of body styles, including a delivery van or even a tow truck.

The Machimoto was an open-top four-wheeler on which the driver and passengers straddled their seats motorcycle style.

The Oldsmobile-powered Incas concept applied similar styling cues to a gull-winged, mid-engined coupe and then Giugiaro went really wild with the Aztec, Aspid and Asgard concepts, which took their biomechanical design theme to such a point that some referred to them as the robocars.

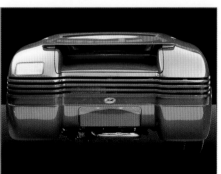

68-69 One writer said Franco Sbarro's Challenge concept looked like a slice of Gruyere cheese. The wedge-shape concept debuted in 1985 at the Geneva show.

69 bottom The rear wing of Franco Sbarro's Challenge acted as an airbrake, which could come in handy when trying to stop a car capable of speeds of 180 miles per hour (300 km/h).

But Giugiaro wasn't alone in exploring radical shapes. Franco Sbarro, a designer born in Italy but based in Switzerland, did everything from his series of wedgy Challenge concepts to the Monster G with huge aircraft wheels and the Osmos which had hubless wheels.

England's IAD (International Automotive Design) studio showed its stunning Alien in 1986, and the vehicle with its curved front compartment and angular power pack truly looked as if it had come to Earth from outer space. IAD followed up with the Impact, Hunter, Interstate and Venus.

Independent design studios weren't alone in their exploration of exotic shapes. Peugeot presented Quasar, Proxima and Oxia. While Quasar and Oxia had names from outer space, Proxima had the most out-of-this-world shape with wheels that almost appear to be detached as they ride below a segmented body.

Citroën's Eole and Activa, Saab's EV-1, Volkswagen's gull-winged Scooter and Matra's P29 and M25 were among the other significant concepts unveiled in Europe.

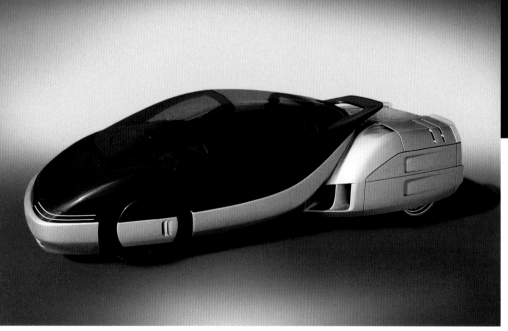

70-71 A concept dated 1986 with out-of-this-world styling was the Peugeot Proxima, which took its name from the star closest to the sun.

70 bottom Although it looked like something from outer space, the Alien was a 1986 concept car from the IAD (International Automotive Design) studio in England.

71 top right Proxima's turbocharged V6 engine had several ceramic components and provided 600 horsepower. The car's minimal frontal design aided the airflow needed to cool the powerful engine.

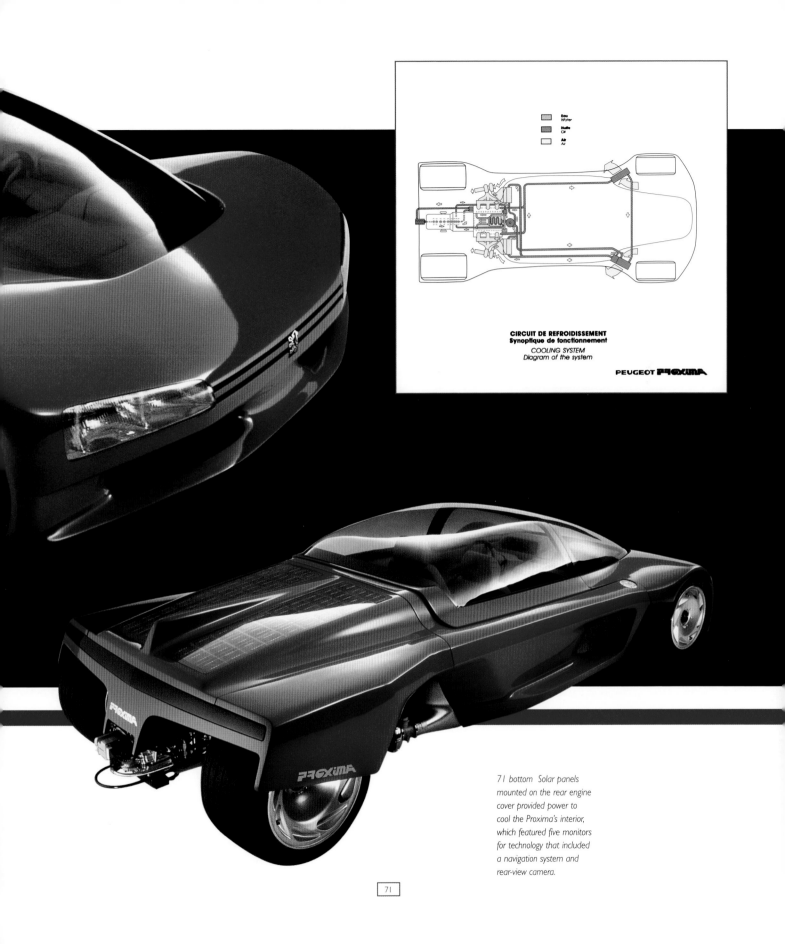

CIRCUIT DE REFROIDISSEMENT
Synoptique de fonctionnement
COOLING SYSTEM
Diagram of the system

PEUGEOT PROXIMA

71 bottom Solar panels mounted on the rear engine cover provided power to cool the Proxima's interior, which featured five monitors for technology that included a navigation system and rear-view camera.

72 top The EV-1 (Experimental Vehicle Number One) was Saab's first concept car. It was unveiled in 1985, and featured several safety innovations. It also had Aramid-reinforced glass fiber body panels that could resume their shape after a minor impact.

72 bottom Solar cells mounted inside the roof panels provided power for a ventilation system to cool the glass-roofed passenger compartment

72-73 Although the EV-1's headlights were small, they were sufficiently powerful to provide the driver with better nighttime illumination.

73 top This drawing from Saab illustrates a new engine program.

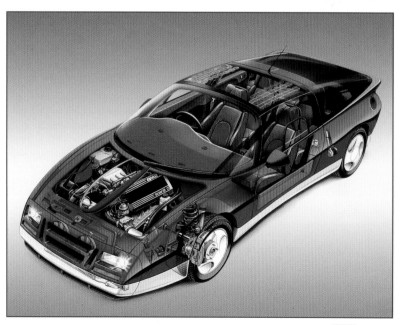

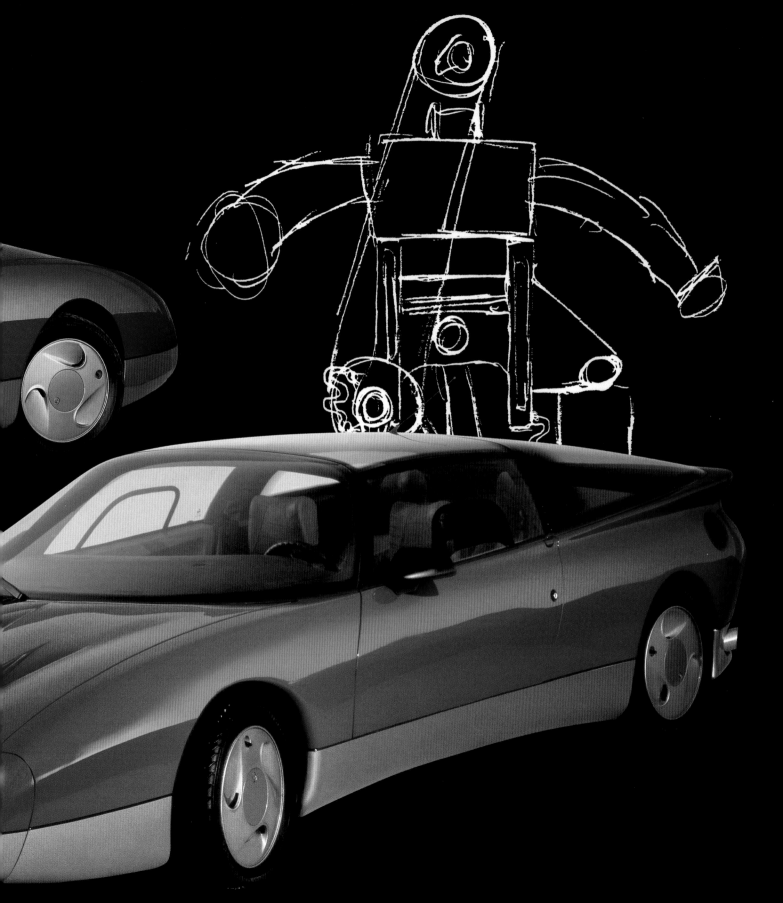

Meanwhile, Chuck Jordan became vice president of GM Design in 1986 and he remembers "my first task was to get excitement back into the business. We'd been held down and everything was conservative." So Jordan called a meeting of his designers and assigned them to create concept vehicles that showed "what we think each division of General Motors should aim for.

"Give them a focus on what we stand for in design," Jordan told his team.

After years of reacting to governmental regulation (a process that included a couple of interesting concept cars that explored aerodynamic shapes) Jordan's department would now take a proactive stance.

The intention, Jordan recalls, was to create design themes to show to the managers of the various GM brands, to provide a starting point for conversations about the future direction of styling.

These concepts were for internal viewing only and the work was being done in secret, with designers enjoying freedom to explore new ideas and design themes… until GM chairman Roger Smith got involved. Although Smith wasn't known as a "car guy," Jordan remembers that he was interested in much more than numbers on balance sheets. One day Smith asked Jordan if he thought GM was going far

74 top After tests at GM's proving grounds, four-time Indy 500 winner A.J. Foyt drove the short-tail Aerotech to a closed course speed record of 275.123 miles per hour and set a "flying mile" mark of 267.399 in the long-tail concept on a test track in Fort Stockton, Texas.

enough with the design of its vehicles. So Jordan took Smith into the skunkworks studios and showed him the cars his designers were creating in secret. By this point, those cars were taking shape in the form of clay models. Smith looked them over, and then went back to his office, leaving Jordan to worry about the chairman's reaction, which came very quickly.

"I got a call that afternoon," Jordan says. "He said, 'hey, I think we ought to finish those cars and have another Motorama. We'll show these cars at the Waldorf'."

The heyday of concept car creation had been sparked by General Motors' Motorama shows, held in

the 1950s and early '60s in the ballroom of New York City's Waldorf-Astoria Hotel, where Harley Earl and his design staff displayed their dream cars. Now concept cars that had been designed for corporate eyes would be seen by thousands of invited guests.

Nicknamed "Rogerama," what was officially labeled "GM Teamwork & Technology — for Today & Tomorrow" was a showcase of General Motors design and technology, and ran for three days in early January 1988 in the ballroom of the Waldorf.

"General Motors was pushing hard to continue to improve fuel economy and quality and we were still struggling coming out of the downturn in the '80s,"

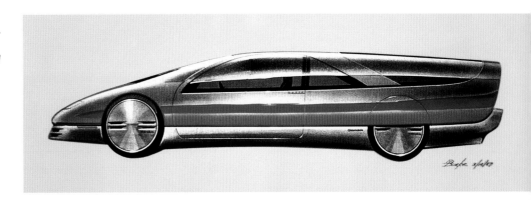

says Larry Faloon, a GM designer who helped organize the Teamwork & Technology show.

"Chuck Jordan was in charge and we'd gotten the idea of a rebirth of interesting concept vehicles. I think we had an enormous positive impact on the General Motors dealers, stakeholders and on the people who had a chance to attend the show. It had been a long, long time since General Motors had really demonstrated in one place the breadth of its technology."

That technology included everything from satellites and a lunar rover to racecars that represented opposite ends of the spectrum of speed and technology: the solar-powered Sunraycer that had just won a race across Australia while the turbocharged engine in the Oldsmobile Aerotech had powered driver A.J. Foyt to closed-course speed records in excess of 275 miles per hour.

"It was a major happening. We took over the entire Waldorf, just like the Motoramas," Faloon remembers. "It opened at 8 a.m. and at 11 p.m. people were still lined up to get in. If you walked out of the south entrance of the Waldorf and looked toward the river, on both sides of the street there was nothing but buses lined up nose to tail."

Concept cars at the show included the Pontiac Banshee, the Buick Lucerne, the GMC Centaur, the Chevrolet Venture, and the show-stopping Cadillac Voyage. Displays included a design studio and modelers who were finishing work on a clay model of a Lotus concept called the Stealth. The Oldsmobile Silhouette concept reportedly was withdrawn virtually on the eve of the show because the company feared it was too early to let its rivals see a design that had been selected to go into series production in just a couple of years.

Several of the GM concepts were shown again 10 days later at the Detroit Auto Show, which a year later itself would be transformed from the Motor City's local dealer show to become one of the world's most important automotive gatherings.

When the concepts went away, so did the excitement," Tom Gale says as he remembers the dark days. "We got into a real fallow period. There was nothing going on." Indeed, at Chrysler, where Gale worked, things were so bad that the firm, one of the world's most prominent automakers, needed the United States federal government to save it from bankruptcy.

"There was no inspiration, no excitement, nothing that would really kind of point the bat at the stands and say, 'I'm going to hit one over there'," says Gale. "That's what the concept cars did for us."

Chrysler desperately needed to make some kind of statement. The Japanese had scored efficiently with small, economical cars and were moving up into other segments of the world's largest automotive market while the Europeans were making strong inroads from the opposite direction.

Meanwhile, Chrysler was building K-Cars, or as Gale correctly notes, by this time in the early and mid 1980s they actually were K-Car derivatives, though that meant they were still little more than boring boxes on wheels. Gale had joined Chrysler after studying engineering and design at a state university, and worked in chassis engineering for several years before moving into the company's styling department.

He became Chrysler's vice president of design in 1985 and retired 15 years later as general manager of all passenger car operations and as executive vice president overseeing Chrysler product design and development.

What he began to develop in the late 1980s was a string of amazing concept vehicles, vehicles that not

CHRYSLER COMES BACK

And so do concept cars

76-77 Lee Iacocca (center) visits the Chrysler design studios in 1984, when many of Chrysler's vehicle's were uninspiring K-Car derivatives. The following year, Tom Gale would be promoted to vice president of design and would use a series of stunning concept cars to re-energize the entire company.

77 bottom Chrysler began its concept car comeback with the Portofino, a car it had begun to show its vision for Lamborghini after it took over the Italian exotic car manufacturer. Portofino made its debut at the Frankfurt show in 1987.

only drove Chrysler's comeback, but vehicles that led other automakers to respond with concept cars of their own.

As a result, the world's major auto shows have become must-attend events that rival Hollywood movie premières or international film festivals in star power and worldwide media coverage.

"The only reason that we decided to get back into concepts after I took over was that it takes a long time for something to come through the production pipeline and the only way we could really try to establish some credibility quickly was to get out there with concepts," Gale explains.

"The [Ford] Taurus and [Mercury] Sable had come out and we were building K-Cars," adds Trevor Creed, who joined Chrysler's design department in 1985 after nearly 20 years with Ford. In the summer of 2000 Creed became Chrysler's senior vice president for design.

"We realized that we had to have a new direc-

tion for the future, that the vehicles had to be more adventurous. We needed to be more revolutionary than any of the future products in the pipeline at Chrysler, and Tom got the go-ahead from Iacocca.

"Lee Iacocca asked Tom, 'are you guys really doing the cars you want?'

" With such encouragement from Chrysler's chairman, "We said, ' why don't we do a series of concept cars to show what our capabilities are for the future?'"

Chrysler's first new concept was the Portofino, which debuted in Frankfurt in 1987.

The car had been conceived as Chrysler's vision for Lamborghini, the famous Italian sports car brand that Chrysler recently had acquired. But while the car still wore the emblem of the Lambo bull when it was unveiled on the auto show stand, the Portofino hinted most directly at the "cab-forward" architecture that would give Chrysler's next generation of production sedans such a boost.

"It said we were capable of doing some things," says Gale. "I can remember Lee Iacocca asked me the question: 'If you can do that with a concept car, why can't we do that with production cars?'"

"You know," Gale responded, "that's really why we do this stuff. That's the question we've been waiting for you to ask."

Gale and his design team began turning out a succession of concept vehicles that not only pushed along future Chrysler production vehicles, but that revitalized and even revolutionized concept car development.

"One of the challenges was that I always wanted to make them out of metal if we could," says Gale.

"Even if the final car was going to be made out of some kind of fiberglass or plastic, making the concepts out of metal looks good.

"Making them run is another good thing. They don't have to be developed. There is no way you're going to develop something in that period of time. But making them run forced you to take a look at cooling

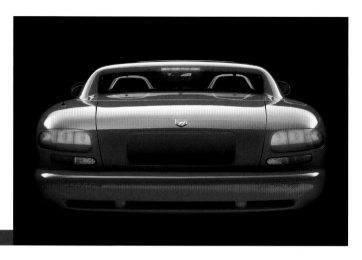

78 top When the Dodge Viper concept was unveiled at the Detroit show in 1989, automotive journalists doubted that Chrysler Corp. could ever build such a vehicle. Their hope was that some specialist company might someday copy the design.

and forced you to take a look at air handling and forced you to take a look at least at some packaging for a cowl and what might later be an HVAC system. That was enough of a link [to a real production vehicle].

"When you look at something that's plywood on the bottom and just fiberglass on top [like many concept cars], there's a certain translation that doesn't happen and they can lose their credibility. They become an art object but they don't really become vehicles. One of the things that was always important for me was to somehow to make them drive onto the display stand and then to be able to make them at least mobile enough that journalists could drive

78-79 and 79 top The V10-powered Dodge Viper did go into production, and on a new Chrysler assembly line in Detroit not very long after a Viper prototype served as the pace car for the 1991 Indianapolis 500.

them and that we could have a way to see what they look like dynamically."

Of course, making concept cars out of metal and equipping them with running gear also made them more expensive.

"One of the things I'm probably the most proud of is that for most of the years that we did this, I never really had the budget," Gale reveals. "I had to go off to beg, borrow or steal that money from marketing, from corporate strategy, from senior management, from wherever. But to show you how supportive everybody was, they coughed up the money and we used to get it done.

"It wasn't until later years that I took control of the budget," he continues. "I didn't really care about the budget. It was more important for me to have the rest of the system support it and to want to put it on the stand."

That way, Gale says, instead of Chrysler's concepts representing his "favorite idea" or some designer's dream, they reflected the aspirations of the corporation's various brands. "We were always very careful to involve the other groups [such as marketing and engineering]. I found that to be very successful and in the end everybody said 'wow, this is what we did.' It created excitement.

"The Viper was a concept car and it provided the face for Dodge. There was the same thing for Chrysler with the winged badge and there was the same thing for Jeep. So were the concepts important? They were something tangible, something you could put your hands on. Man, I think they were terribly important."

And that excitement spread not only throughout Chrysler, but throughout the industry.

"There's no doubt about it," Gale says. "Concept cars weren't a new idea. Harley Earl and Bill Mitchell did them for years [at General Motors] and [Virgil] Exner did them for years [at Chrysler]. But it was just an opportunity in the mid '80s that nobody else was doing them.

GM had started to do it; Charlie Jordan did a great job with some of the cars [for GM's Teamwork and Technology show].

But when we decided to jump in with both feet they stayed out and Ford stayed out."

It wasn't until the early '90s that people started coming back into it.

"I can remember meeting with the guys who were the promoters of the Detroit auto show in the late '80s. I said we'd get behind it, that I'd do my best to make sure we'd debut our stuff at Detroit, and it really did get the ball rolling. At first that ball rolled in some very unusual directions.

"We started out doing things like Sling Shot and car within a car and really wacky stuff," Gale remembers. "When you look back, for example, in the '50s

and stuff would look like an F85 Sabre jet. That's fine, but it was never very predictive."

Sling Shot was wedge-shaped sports car with wide wheels enclosed in even wider, tube-like fenders that extended from the body, the front wheels just below the rear view mirrors and the rear wheels at the very rear edge of the car.

Car-within-a-car was the Voyager III, which looked as if one vehicle has swallowed another, which was pretty much the idea: The front half of the car was a three-passenger vehicle that could separate from a tail trailer section that provided seating for as many as eight people. Trevor Creed remembers that the studio decided that instead of using current production platforms, "We'd do something way out there and advanced looking and yet we were doing that for an auto show but we wouldn't dream of doing that for production.

"What's wrong with this picture? From that came the next series of vehicles that were precursors. "When you have a new design coming out that you're proud of, it is not a bad idea rather than to wait until

right to the last minute and say 'boom, there it is and now you can buy it,' but there is some value in getting out ahead of the introduction of the vehicle with a mildly disguised, almost 95 percent of the vehicle, as we did with the Pacifica.

"We call it a concept car, but I think that's probably a mistake. The dream cars that GM did in those days were kind of one-off design studies that they had no intention of building.

"In our case we may do a project like that, which we've code-named blue sky. Those GM concepts cars were real blue sky."

"The concept cars that people build these days, including ourselves, you guys in the media don't say, 'well, are you going to built it?' as much as you say, 'when are you going to built it?' because there's such a level of credibility there.

"So in a way we need to do a little bit of blue-sky stuff that pushes the boundaries.

"It's fun for our designers. It demonstrates your designers' capabilities and it's an extreme morale-booster for the studio."

80 top The 1990 Chrysler Voyager III was an interesting if impractical concept for a minivan. The front portion was a separate three-passenger city car powered by a four-cylinder engine.

80-81 bottom The rear section of the Voyager III provided seating for up to eight passengers. It also had its own four-cylinder engine to power the rear wheels when the two sections were linked together.

"It's fun to do. It's fun to test the limits," Gale resumes. "But we had a stronger response from the public with the things that they could make the connection, that they could say, 'Oh, yes, I can see where this connects to that and maybe with some work this is something that's going to happen. I can understand why you take out the B pillar and the doors do this and I can understand why you might want to do that.'

"In the end, the media and the public, their reaction to things drove this to come to a more developed stance, and that's harder to do, but it's going to have benefits. Many of the concepts we did helped us to get our production vehicles to reach a little further."

Few vehicles reached as far as the Dodge Viper sports car concept did in 1989 at Detroit or as the Plymouth Prowler, a factory-built hot-rod concept, did four years later in the same venue. Both of those made the most amazing reach — from almost cartoon-like, schoolboy's doodle concept car to production vehicle.

82-83 The Plymouth Prowler, with styling inspired by the classic American hot rod, debuted as a concept car at the Detroit show in 1993. Like the Viper, the Prowler was so well received on the auto show circuit that a production version was launched. The V6-powered Plymouth Prowler made its debut as a 1997 model. Although the Plymouth brand was dropped from the lineup, the factory-built hot rod stayed in production as the Chrysler Prowler until the winter of 2002.

Chrysler's concepts continue to push its mainstream production vehicles to places far beyond where anyone might have expected from a company going nowhere with K-Cars, expect for going bankrupt. You may not (yet) be able to park an Atlantic or a Chronos, a Copperhead or a Venom, an M80 or Powerbox in your garage. Maybe you wouldn't want to be seen in the Super 8 Hemi, the car former Chrysler executive Bob Lutz compared to a toaster

on wheels. But recall that the Pronto Cruiser, presented at an auto show as just the packaging around a new powertrain, turned out to be the "segment busting" PT Cruiser, or that the Crossfire and Pacifica concepts are rolling little changed from show stands to show rooms.

Chrysler powered its comeback with concept cars, and now many of those show cars have become go cars.

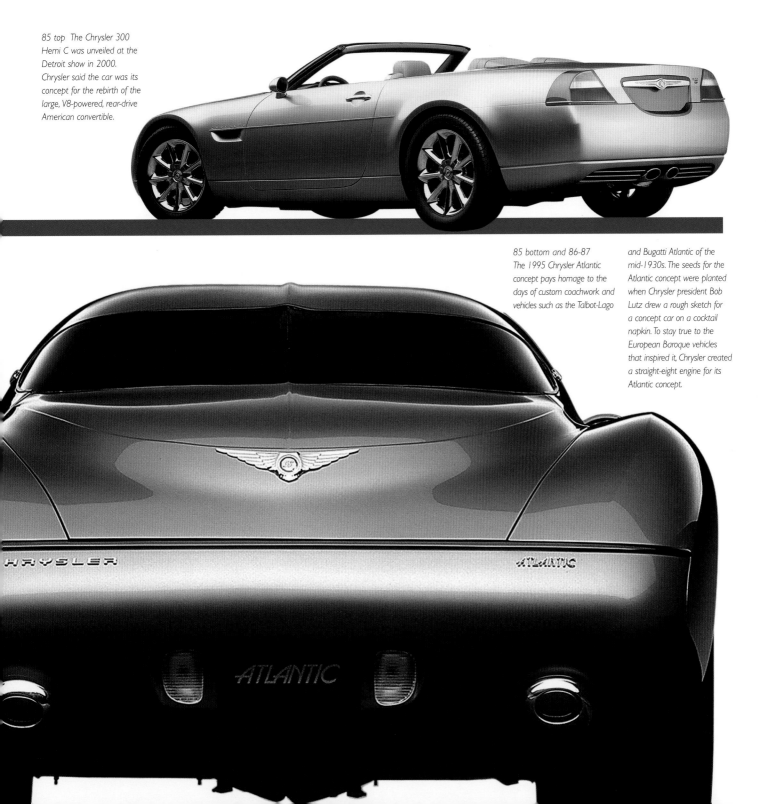

85 top The Chrysler 300 Hemi C was unveiled at the Detroit show in 2000. Chrysler said the car was its concept for the rebirth of the large, V8-powered, rear-drive American convertible.

85 bottom and 86-87 The 1995 Chrysler Atlantic concept pays homage to the days of custom coachwork and vehicles such as the Talbot-Lago and Bugatti Atlantic of the mid-1930s. The seeds for the Atlantic concept were planted when Chrysler president Bob Lutz drew a rough sketch for a concept car on a cocktail napkin. To stay true to the European Baroque vehicles that inspired it, Chrysler created a straight-eight engine for its Atlantic concept.

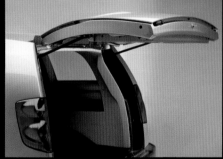

88 The 2001 Dodge Super8 Hemi was designed to apply styling cues from modern trucks and sport utility vehicles to a classic American family sedan.

The Super8 Hemi may have '50s-style bench seats, but it also offers such modern technology as touch-screen Internet access for those sitting on the back bench.

89 top The 2001 Dodge PowerBox is a sport utility vehicle concept with a rugged look but also with an environmentally friendly compressed natural gas and electric hybrid powertrain.

89 bottom The PowerBox introduced the "combogate." The rear hatch can be opened as a liftgate or can serve as a tailgate to extend the vehicle's cargo-carrying floor.

FREEMAN THOMAS

Rebel with a cause

90-91 Freeman Thomas and J Mays were co-conspirators in the design of the Concept 1. Public reaction was so strong that 11 months later Volkswagen announced plans to put the New Beetle into production.

91 right In 1995, Freeman Thomas designed the Audi TT and TTS Spyder concepts that would lead to the production of the Audi TT coupe and roadster.

"In its pure act," says Freeman Thomas, "design is a rebellious act. It's one of contempt. It's one of challenge. It's one of defying the status quo."

Not every automotive designer gets to practice the art in such a pure form, but Freeman Thomas has built his career around defying the status quo, around the rebellious experimentation that can produce breathtaking concept vehicles, vehicles that sometimes make the remarkable breakthrough from concept to production. Take, for example, the Volkswagen New Beetle, which was designed by Thomas and co-conspirator J Mays.

"Did Volkswagen want to do another Beetle?" Thomas repeats the question. "Not at all.

"We were taking advantage of the fact that [VW chairman] Ferdinand Piech was the grandson of Ferdinand Porsche [creator of the original Beetle]. We were taking advantage of the fact that Piech was new to his job and was looking for a stage to stand on.

"We were taking advantage of the fact that Ferdinand Piech was looking for diversion from his scandal [the infamous Inaki Lopez case]. And as designers, we saw that Volkswagen was ready to pull out of the American market.

"All of these negative things were the tools that created something positive. Had those negative things not been going on, they wouldn't have listened to us."

But VW did listen. It really didn't have much choice, especially not after the Concept 1 show car became such an immediate and huge hit on the auto show circuit. Concept 1 made its debut at Detroit in January 1994. In November of that same year VW announced plans to put the New Beetle into produc-

tion. The rebels had won.

Once again, Volkswagen drove to success in a car that defied the norm. After creating such breakthrough concepts as the Audi Avus and VW Concept 1, Mays moved his rebellion to Ford, where he became vice president of design and perhaps the best-known American car designer since Harley Earl. After the New Beetle, Thomas did the concepts that would beget the revolutionary Audi TT coupe and roadster, and then joined Chrysler, first as vice president of advanced product design strategy at corporate headquarters in Auburn Hills, Michigan (an in-house rebel with a cause), though he didn't stay long at HQ.

Within a year he was posted to Pacifica.

Pacifica is DaimlerChrysler's dream factory, its design studio in southern California.

"I'm a California boy," says Thomas, who was born in the sun in the summer of 1957, attended the Art Center College of Design in Pasadena and then went to work after college at Porsche, where he was part of the team that designed the revolutionary 959 supercar. For Freeman Thomas, coming to Pacifica was coming home. But it was more than that, it was a rebel's dream come true.

"What I love about out here is the autonomy and the distance [from the home office]. It actually gives us more credibility. We're inside the company but we're outside the company. We get to be an outside voice, almost like a rudder of the ship. It's kind of like this space station that everyone wants to come to." "The Pacifica guys are out of the timing plan," design chief Trevor Creed says of Chrysler's strict styling timelines. "They're free, if you will, to fail."

"We have projects in the back room that are ideas that are really good solutions for the [Chrysler] brands, for what could be their next vehicles, and we have ideas that are planned for different auto shows that are really out there, things that even if you were to put that project into a design school, the students would look conservative by comparison," says Thomas. What challenges his designers, Thomas says, is anticipating technology.

"A car is made up of hundreds of developments of different types of technology, from lighting systems to drivetrain systems to seating systems to steering systems and on and on and on," he explains. "It's when you combine these ideas together and put them with a lifestyle… that it becomes aspirational. It's taking a combination of these new developments and combining them together in unique and original ways. We

work closely with our advanced engineering groups, like Liberty and Mercedes and our Palo Alto group, and we see what kind of new developments they have on the drawing boards and then we start having discussions and say, 'hey, we have a great idea for a vehicle that could help you tell that story, to describe that technology, whether it's for a near-term vehicle or something that's more blue sky.'

"The near-term vehicle uses technology that is on the shelf, that is fairly easy to apply and that communicates to an audience that says that's what we would like to buy next."

"But blue-sky vehicle concepts," he says, "look ahead, sometimes even 10 years into the future, and Thomas reminds us that in 10 years portable telephones went from being large, cumbersome briefcase-sized boxes to micro-sized cell phones that can communicate not only by voice but via the Internet, which, he notes, wasn't available a decade ago to the civilian population.

Thomas says that what his designers need to be is what he calls cultural architects. "For me, being a cultural architect is being a visionary and being able to take events, somehow connected or disconnected, and to put them together into a happening that effects culture. In this case it's the automobile, or the way that we transport people.

"That's how, I think, if you're challenged with a packaging problem and you say, 'I have a good intuition that's based on previous experiences that technology in this area is going to get smaller and more refined and in 10 years the package will be this size,' so you make assumptions for packaging spaces of certain things.

"In a blue-sky project, you make these assumptions and by the time you're done, you have a vehicle that you hopefully want to maximize the room for the people and minimize the amount of space for componentry. I think the computer and cell phones are great examples of where things have gone." Another example, he suggests, is television, which as gone from big tubes to thin, plasma screens. Thomas says it won't be long before instead of sitting on a piece of furniture, a TV may be a curtain that retracts into a wall.

"All of our ideas, even our blue-sky ones, I want them to have logic," Thomas explains. "If you're por-

traying a future transportation scenario, even if the technology isn't up to speed yet, have logic so that by the time you're proposing this vehicle, the technology will be there. At the end, it has to be real, not just be perceived. But a concept vehicle still can ask questions. It can be fantasy."

Some people might see such fantasy as failure, but Thomas says that the fun really begins when Pacifica has designed a vehicle that doesn't seem to fit within Chrysler's portfolio of brands.

"The fun ones," he says, "those are the ones that challenge the brand." For example, consider that the Chrysler PT Cruiser — which didn't seem to fit into any segment, let alone any brand — had an invigorating impact on the Chrysler much as the New Beetle did on Volkswagen.

92-93 Although they sometimes are dismissed as mere model makers, the craftsmen who work on this full-scale clay model in Chrysler's Pacifica studio are skilled sculptors.

93 top John Sodano sketches in Chrysler's Pacifica studio, which is managed by Freeman Thomas. Sodano and Chris Schuttera designed the interior for the Dodge Razor concept car while Akino Tsuchiya and Kevin Verduyn did that concept's exterior design.

93 bottom The Dodge Viper concept car takes shape as a three-dimensional clay model in Chrysler's Pacifica studio.

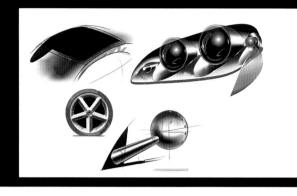

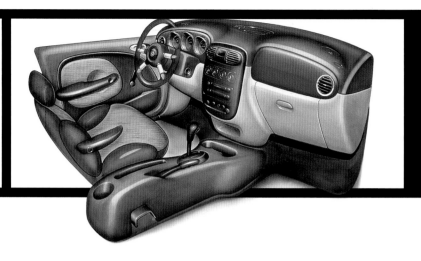

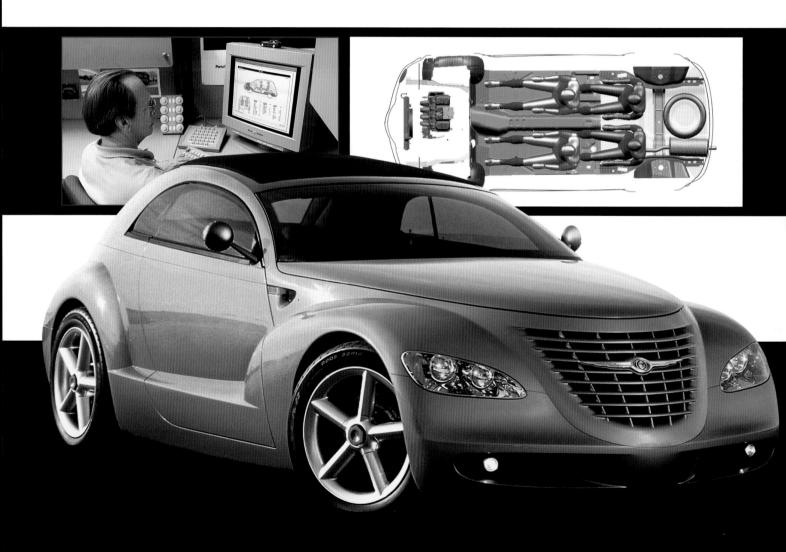

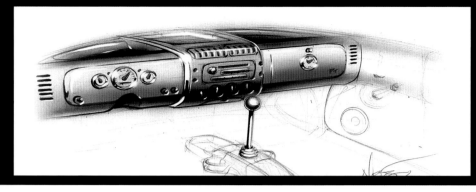

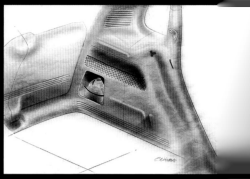

94 People may live inside their cars, but it is a vehicle's exterior that first catches the eye. Designers are given freedom to dream of the most appealing lines and shapes as they make their preliminary sketches of new vehicles. What people noticed about the Pronto Cruizer was its design, not its powertrain, and the popular concept was transformed into the Chrysler PT Cruiser production vehicle for the 2001 model year.

95 top Designers aren't the only people you'll find behind the locked doors of places such as Chrysler's Pacifica studio. The staff includes skilled model makers and a group of automotive engineers who work with the designers to make sure that their designs have real-world manufacturing feasibility.

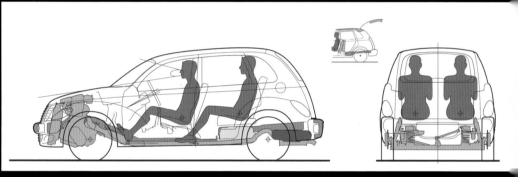

95 center and bottom The Pronto Cruizer was a Chrysler concept vehicle shown at Geneva in 1998, where it was meant to draw attention to its engine, a new joint-venture project between Chrysler and BMW. With people spending more time in their vehicles, interior design becomes more important, especially as designers try to meet customer expectations for intuitive controls and "infotainment" technologies as well as improvements in vehicle safety features.

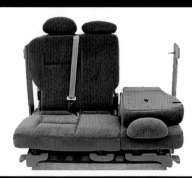

"With concept cars," Thomas continues, "we started experimenting with the Jeep brand. On one end you might have the Willys2 [a modern interpretation of the original Willy's G.I. transporter] and on the other end you might have the Compass [a cross between a Jeep and a rally car, designed for the post-Baby Boom generation and inspired by yet another Jeep concept, an off-road sports car called the Jeepster]."

They are two completely different types of vehicles, but are either of them less Jeep?

"That's something we challenge ourselves with, that's why we do those types of things as concept vehicles, to weigh them before we do something as a production vehicle.

"If you look at the Wrangler, that's something that's a tried-and-true Jeep product. But before it became a tried-and-true Jeep product it was a military product. But it became a Jeep product. It earned that position. In a sense that's what our concept vehicles do. These are the opportunities, and we allow ourselves to be creative, to take chances, to take risks." But even a rebel may set some limits around those risks.

"It's all done in the context of the story of the brand," Thomas explains. "That's really what your umbrella is. Coming from Europe and truly great brands, and looking at the brands of the Chrysler Group, when I think of Jeep that's what it is, it's the brand. You're a curator of a great brand.

"Take Harley-Davidson or BMW or Mercedes. If you take the brand away from the equation, you're just executing a functional device. The brand

aspect is the emotional, philosophical part of it, it's what separates a BMW from a Mercedes is the philosophy, the art, the history, the part that says that at Mercedes we do it this way and at BMW we do it this way. I love that.

"As a brand you want to show your independence, and that's what concept cars do very well, they teach and educate the public of what the brand's potentials are."

96 top and 97 top and right Designers use concept cars to demonstrate how a specific brand might expand its range. Freeman Thomas suggests that this is the case when designers presented Jeep with the Compass (left) and the Willys2

(right). The Jeep Willys2 debuted at Tokyo in 2001, where it was presented as a modern interpretation of the classic Jeep. Unveiled at Detroit in 2002, the Compass uses rally-car styling cues to create a hip, urban twist on the Jeep heritage.

96-97 Chrysler's Pacifica studio not only designed this concept, but gave its name to the vehicle that Chrysler said followed its original minivan and its PT Cruiser in creating an entirely new segment — the sports tourer. The Pacifica combines elements of a car, a minivan and an SUV. The concept was introduced in 2002 and a production version was launched for the 2004 model year.

THE DREAM FACTORY

 A concept car begins as a designer's dream. That dream is conceived as an image, sometimes just a few preliminary lines and shapes made on paper or a computer screen. But a concept car isn't just a dreamy drawing. Even in its most rudimentary form, it's a three-dimensional — if stationary — sculpture made of clay and fiberglass. But to truly become a dream machine, a concept car must be a machine, and that requires that the designer's dream take shape in metal and glass, plastics and rubber and leather, and with computerized controls for its electrical and other operating systems.

This transformation from designer's dream to rolling reality requires hours of labor by designers, engineers and highly skilled craftsmen and women.

The world's major automakers are used to building cars in series of tens and hundreds of thousands, using gigantic stamping presses and long lines with robotic welders and blood and sweat assembly line workers who produce vehicles designed for use by fleets and families.

But one-of-a-kind concept cars require the expertise of specialists, often craftsmen and women whose skills range from those used in the earliest days of customized coach building, with panels pounded into shape by hand over a wooden frame or carefully curved by a craftsman on an English wheel, to those requiring cutting-edge capabilities in such things as computer-aided manufacturing, carbon fiber molding and glassmaking.

Such wide-ranging expertise is concentrated in only a few places on the planet. As might be expect-

ed, these skills can be found in Turin, in Detroit and in some of the other major automotive centers. But they have been developed to a special state in a much more unlikely location, in a complex of workshops behind a nondescript office building that sits across the street from strawberry fields in Fountain Valley, California. With tall trees lining the curb along Slater Avenue and with a narrow parking lot providing an additional buffer, most people driving past probably

How designers' dreams take shape as mobile, metal masterpiece

don't even notice the white, two-story building with its mirrored glass windows, and it would take a sharp eye to read the small sign above the front door:

The Gaffoglio Family

Metalcrafters

AUTOMOBILE BODY MAKERS

"Automobile body makers" conjures up images of heavy industry, a stamping plant that uses huge dies to pound flat sheets of steel or aluminum into fenders and doors and roof panels, which are welded together to form automobile body shells, oddly shaped and hollow metal structures awaiting the engines and electronics and tires and interiors that transform them into motor vehicles. Indeed, the Metalcrafters workshops have a newly installed, 1,800-ton stamping press that can shape a steel sheet into a complexly curved panel.

98 and 99 top To turn a designer's sketches into a concept car such as the Dodge Razor (far left and above) requires thousands of steps. Photos taken during the Razor's creation show the full-size clay model (top), that model being painted for corporate approval (center) before a metal version of the concept is built for the auto show circuit (bottom).

99 bottom The men behind the metal: (from left) Ruben, George, John, and Marcelo Gaffoglio and Michael Alexander have built Metalcrafters into one of the world's leading concept car constructors.

There also is a new glass-bending facility that is the envy even of Turin's concept car builders.

"We have the latest technology. We believe strongly in technology," says George Gaffoglio. "But we can go back 100 years and do it the old-fashioned way with the English wheel and hammers. We're taking coach building to the space age. It's the combination of those two that is the essence of Metalcrafters."

Metalcrafters was founded by John Gaffoglio, who was born in Argentina but whose grandparents emigrated from Italy. John and his bride immigrated to the United States, to southern California, in the mid-1960s. But she missed her family, went home for vacation and convinced John to move back. But he took with him modern American tools, hand- and power-tools that weren't available in Argentina, tools that he and a cousin used to build a successful auto-body repair business. But in 1973, as Argentina suffered political and economic turmoil, John Gaffoglio lost everything but his family and his experience, with

which he returned to California, where he, his 15-year-old son George and 14-year-old son Ruben went to work in a succession of car dealerships and body shops.

But they kept getting fired, John recalls, because "our way of doing things was very different from the 'American way'." Americans were in a hurry, preferring to go out and buy a new part rather than repair the old one. "I fixed things the old-fashioned way — with my own two hands," John explains. "I quickly realized that if I wanted to work the way I had been taught [and the way he, in turn, had taught his sons], we would have to start our own business."

That business would be well served by the Gaffoglios' steadfast dedication to combining old world craftsmanship with new world technology.

Metalcrafters was established to do body repairs, especially on exotic sports cars, and became known for converting Ferrari Daytona coupes into Spyder convertibles, and for preparing vehicles for use in Hollywood movies. Chrysler hired Metalcrafters to

build the prototypes for its K-Car, and to do convertible conversions after the K-Car went into production. That relationship expanded into building concept cars for Chrysler, and subsequently for many of the world's other automakers.

The Metalcrafters managing family includes John Gaffoglio, his sons George, Ruben, Marcelo and Eric, as well as Michael Alexander, who may not have come from the Gaffoglio family tree, and who came to the Gaffoglios from a career in aerospace construction management and with roots that are deeply automotive. Alexander's father and uncle were the Alexander Brothers, famed custom car builders in Detroit.

The Gaffoglios and Alexander run a company with more than 200 engineers, project managers, designers, crafts specialists and others who work two shifts a day in three buildings that span 160,000 square feet of floor space. To protect the privacy of clients who may spend more than $2 million on a concept car that must remain well-hidden until its

unveiling on a show stand half way around the world, the facility is surrounded by tall fences and locked gates. Once inside those gates, you need to know the various locking codes for the doors that lead into hallways. But even after you gain access to those hallways, all you see are doors with more codes that protect the work of the various departments, whether it's the room where design details are being expanded on a computer screen or the shop where the 40 separate pieces needed to create a functioning taillight are being assembled so they can be taken behind yet another locked door to be installed on a concept car.

"Security is the No. 1 tool," says George Gaffoglio as he points out some of the 120 closed-circuit television cameras that monitor the entire facility. The security system works so well, he adds, that John Gaffoglio once caught one of his sons smoking after he's sworn that he'd quit."

While a concept car may start with a single sketch, to convert that sketch into a drivable machine can require the design and creation of thousands or parts and pieces. Each car, says George Gaffoglio, involves "800 major steps, and each step probably has 10 other sub-steps." Eight hundred times 10 are 8,000 steps per vehicle, and Metalcrafters handles as many as 10 concept car projects simultaneously.

"Designers are very sensitive about their vehicles and what they want executed," says Don Bradley, Chrysler Group's manager of specialty and concept vehicle engineering and the company's primary liaison with Metalcrafters during the concept car construction process. "Metalcrafters has demonstrated historically that they're able to execute what the design staff intended. Their level of execution is a stop above everything else."

"Concept cars are masterpieces," says George Gaffoglio. "The clients create the masterpieces. The car looks good because of the design the customer does. We bring in the quality of the craftsmanship. The design, the idea comes from the client. It's up to

100-101 Razor's designers were inspired by the minimalist cues of European sports cars of the 1960s, although their modern update displays an aggressive American attitude. The

Razor takes its name from the Razor scooter, which challenged the skateboard as the favorite method of self-propelled transportation for Americans too young to drive.

us to execute, and in 18-20 weeks."

So how is a concept car executed? Well, the process starts long before Metalcrafters ever sets hammer to metal: The process from designer's dream to show stand reality can take more than a year, or as few as a few weeks, depending on the automaker involved in the project.

Chrysler follows a very disciplined time line that starts every year, usually in late fall, when a call goes out from the vice president of design, Trevor Creed. After they hear presentations from Chrysler's marketing department about the company's various

brands and from engineering about its newest technologies, Creed asks the design staff a couple of seemingly simple questions and gives one basic instruction: "What's missing from our portfolio?" and "What don't we build that you would love to own?" he asks.

Then he adds what can be a daunting instruction: "Just sketch up something that you think would be great in the marketplace."

Those sketches will be displayed on in a room in Chrysler's headquarters at Auburn Hills, Michigan. The room is known as Area 51, just like top-secret aerospace test site in Nevada. But instead of stealth bombers and who knows what sort of concept air-

do a Cadillac pickup truck, because you're trashing the brand, and we're very proud of our brands," he adds, enjoying the jab at cross-town rival General Motors and its new Cadillac-branded pickup truck. Still, part of the fun of concept cars is how they can expand the brand and its appeal. For example, consider how the Chrysler brand widened when it presented the Pronto Cruizer concept at Geneva in 1998 and later launched a production vehicle called the PT Cruiser.

So Creed doesn't reject an idea without hearing from the designer behind it. "In my day, you put up all of your stuff but you were not allowed to be there," he says, recalling his years at Ford in Europe.

that don't exist. It just comes right out of somebody's head. It's a real challenge."

Part of that challenge is creating a story around a car, or a group of cars, such as the trio of concepts Chrysler showed in 2001 at the North American International Auto Show in Detroit.

Those cars were the Dodge Razor, the Jeep Compass and the Dodge M80, all small and affordable vehicles designed for the so-called millennial generation, much of which was still much too young to have driver's licenses.

"We'll put a price tag on something," Freeman Thomas says of the research that goes into vehicle design, even into concept cars. "That focuses us to

craft making test flights under the cover of darkness, Chrysler's secret Area 51 contains its secret showcase the group's brands — Chrysler, Dodge, Dodge truck and Jeep — the past, present and even future generations of their lineup of vehicles as well as their recent concept cars and now the designers' proposals for new concepts.

"'There's no way that's a Chrysler. Take it down," Creed may say when he sees what appears to be a Jeep placed on the Chrysler board. "There's a tendency," he explains, "to think that because the Chrysler brand doesn't have a Jeep-like vehicle, it needs one. But we don't do a Chrysler Jeep any more than you

"The chief designer or executive would review all of the sketches and at the end all you would know is that he didn't pick anything or he picked this one.

"We allow each of our designers to present the sketches, to explain what he or she was thinking.

"It's a real challenge to have somebody come up with something that doesn't exist," Creed explains. "It's like the kid in *The Sixth Sense*, the movie, who said, 'I see dead people.' We see cars that don't exist. That's the difference between us and an artist. An artist is somebody who looks at something and paints a picture of it.

"He can reproduce something. But we do things

creatively come up with solutions that are justified within that price class, so we're not trying to create something that you look at and say, 'they'd never be able to do that'.

"So when we put down our $15,000 price tag for an M80 pickup or a Razor sports car, we were realistic in our internal discussions in saying, 'yes, we can do this.' 'O.K., maybe we're a little over the top on this thing or that, but it's a concept car and we can do that a little bit.' It's like going into a model home and saying 'I know my house is not going to have that view…'"

But the designers must do their homework. For

example, the Razor concept wasn't equipped with a radio, because its designers knew that the first thing young buyers do is to remove the original audio equipment so they can install their own system, customized to their personal tastes.

"We put a tremendous amount of research into these vehicles," Creed explains. Another example is the four-point seat belt system used in the Razor. "Unlike our generation that had no seat belts or that fastened them behind your back and sat on them because of [the irritating noise of] the warning chimes and today wears them reluctantly because we were a generation that as children were rolling around on the back seat, this generation was brought up in car

managers and schedulers create a computer-generated flow chart that covers each of those steps, and with so many steps, each flow chart is large enough to cover a large conference table or an entire office wall.

Every part and piece must be designed and built, molded or fabricated, painted or polished. Sub-assemblies are assembled and mounted into the body of a vehicle that gone through its own development, from sketch to clay model that provides surface data so metal can be shaped into a brightly painted body with a complete and functioning and upholstered and wood- or metal-trimmed interior.

Metalcrafters may not be a heavy industrial com-

advanced glass-shaping facility in the world.

What Metalcrafters builds may look like beautiful automotive sculpture, but these vehicles are much more, they are concept cars, cars and trucks and minivans and sport utilities that are not just for show, but also for go.

They are built to withstand the rigors of Metalcrafters' own shakedown drive on a test track, to stand up to toil of international travel and handling by truckers and auto show workers.

Surviving all that, they finally face perhaps their toughest test, the sometimes not so careful driving by automotive journalists in pursuit of magazine cover stories.

seats. Mom and dad fastened them in. I think they think the whole thing of fastening seat belts is cool, and especially the guys because they associate it with racing. So we had our four-point belts, no radios, and we kept the controls simple… with roll down windows, which fascinate this generation."

The concepts that make the cut are presented to Chrysler's upper management for approval, designs are refined and stories crafted. Then Chrysler turns to Metalcrafters for the 8,000 steps needed to convert sketched dreams and storylines into sheetmetal reality.

For each concept vehicle, Metalcrafters project

plex on the order of one of the major automakers, but it does everything needed to build a car except powertrain development and tire molding. It has five-axis lasers and five-axis mills and various stamping presses and makes its own dies for those presses and mills its own wheels and constructs full chassis and bodies and the complete interiors. Its laminating shop and autoclave work with advanced composites — and not just for concept cars; Metalcrafters produces lightweight, one-piece carbon-fiber bodies for drag-racing's fastest Funny Cars. It also fabricates suspension components, electrical, lighting and other mechanical systems and has perhaps the most

102 and 102-103 The theme behind the Dodge MAXXcab concept was to put the priority on the people inside, because many Americans drive trucks instead of cars on a daily basis. For the 2000 Detroit show, Metalcrafters built the Dodge MAXXcab, Chrysler 300 Hemi C, Jeep Varsity and Chrysler Panel Cruiser concept vehicles.

103 right The Dodge M80, a compact four-wheel-drive pickup truck, takes its name from a firecracker. It's designed to appeal to the same millennial generation as the Razor coupe.

CALIFORNIA DREAMIN'

AND DESIGNIN'

While the American car companies and their designers were struggling with new government regulations, the Japanese were exporting both their small, fuel-efficient cars and their talented young designers to the West Coast of the United States.

The designers arrived to study at the Art Center College of Design in Pasadena, California, where many, perhaps even most of the world's leading automotive designers have done their academic studies before moving into carmakers' studios.

Strother MacMinn began working in Harley Earl's studios at General Motors in 1936, but left soon after World War II to return to Pasadena, his hometown, where he taught at Art Center for some five decades.

"Strother MacMinn was approached by Toyota. He had been responsible for teaching and educating so much of their staff, and they said they would like to have a temporary studio and to have somebody to teach their staff in European and American design methodology," recalls David Stollery, who was recruited by MacMinn to establish Toyota's Calty studio.

Calty, short for California Toyota, set the pattern for other West Coast design studios — Japanese, European and domestic — by providing both a base for design work as well as a research center for studying the trend-setting edge of the largest car market on the planet.

"I think culturally the car represents something different to the Japanese than it does to Americans,"

104-105 In addition to designs from their own studios, automakers often sponsor projects by student designers. Bob Mochizuki was studying at the Art Center College of Design

when he did this concept for an Acura-badged pickup truck. This compact and sporty vehicle has a reconfigurable bed with a hard cover that folds into the truck's side panels.

105 right Skilled hands are needed for the design of concept cars and for the construction of the scale models built for three-dimensional evaluation of those designs.

notes Dan Sims, design director at Mitsubishi's West Coast studio.

"The car has been such an integral part of American history from the early 1900s on, from the way the Model T basically transformed the nation to how recent urban planning has been so influenced by the automobile. It's undeniable.

"And the automobile arrived at the point where we were expanding westward. We didn't have villages that had been here since the Middle Ages like in Europe or Japan. The car drove the development of our cities, for better or worse. Los Angeles was the epitome of that."

"I was brought up in LA, and there was no art of any kind," says C. Edson Armi, a professor of art history at the University of California Santa Barbara, where the courses he teaches range from medieval architecture and sculpture to modern design as well as a seminar on automotive design.

Armi recalls that if you grew up in Los Angeles and "if you were interested in visual things, you were focused on cars on the freeway." He remembers playing a game with his brother; the winner was the first one to identify 10 consecutive years of any model of car.

Southern California's close connection to the car was portrayed around the world in Hollywood movies and in songs about the *Little Old Lady from Pasadena* and how we can have "fun fun fun 'til her daddy takes the T-Bird away." Southern California is the home of the hot rod, and of the drive-thru,

drive-in and even the drive-by. Like C. Edson Armi, David Stollery grew up in southern California, where his first career was that of childhood actor, working for Walt Disney's studios and gaining fame as Marty in the television serial *Spin and Marty*. Despite such early success in show business, Stollery wasn't interested in a career in the movies or television.

"Girls want to be fashion models and boys want to be car designers or rock stars," Stollery says, recalling his teenage environment in southern California. "I couldn't sing or play the guitar, so I went over to cars."

Stollery studied at Art Center, and then worked in Europe — in both Germany and Italy — and in Detroit, for General Motors, where he managed Chevrolet's advanced design studio before

he returned to southern California at the age of 30.

"I was old enough to have the experience, but was still young enough to be considered creative and energetic," Stollery recalls of MacMinn's introduction of Stollery to Toyota.

Toyota offered Stollery a two-year contract "to set up a little, temporary studio.

"They would send over their people. I would train them. They felt that in a couple of years they would have all the training they needed and they would go away.

"But over that two years they realized that this was an on-going process," Stollery adds, noting that both he and his staff were constantly learning new procedures and methodologies and that "this was never going to stop and they realized they needed

106 top and 107 top Designers gather to consider interior options for a concept car created at Toyota's Calty studio. Modern computers provide a virtual, three-dimensional view of a designer's work. But to fully appreciate a design, it needs to be created in the form of a scale model, and then in a full-size perspective

to make it permanent."

Stollery worked at Calty for seven years, then left and set up his own design consulting company. Renault approached him about establishing a West Coast studio for the French automaker, but he declined. "I already knew what was going to happen," he says, "I'd set it up and be the guy working until midnights and on weekends, and when I get everything running, their management will be set up above me."

Instead, he set up his own company, to consult for Renault and many others. Work by his Industrial Design Research includes car designs for automakers around the world — and especially for those in emerging markets — as well as Stollery's own Arex concept car, the new monorail system being built in Las Vegas, a Class A semi-type truck, and the design and manufacture of fiberglass lifeguard observation towers and shelters that dot beaches from Florida to Hawaii. He also teaches classes at Art Center.

Stollery opened Calty opened in 1973. In 1974 Toyota surpassed Volkswagen in sales to become the No. 1 importer in the American automotive market. Coincidence? Certainly, but in 1978 the Stollery-designed Celica was considered a breakthrough car for Toyota.

Such success, by Toyota and by its California design studio, drew attention, especially in Japan but also around the world.

Suddenly, Stollery recalls, "Everybody had to have one," a design base of their own in southern California. "The next one was Nissan's, down in La Jolla [just north of San Diego]."

Others would follow and, as Stollery notes, "Now everyone has a studio." Indeed, Audi/ Volkswagen (Santa Monica), BMW (Newbury Park), DaimlerChrysler (Carlsbad), Ford (Valencia), General Motors (North Hollywood), Honda (Torrance), Hyundai (Fountain Valley), Isuzu (Cerritos), Mazda (Irvine), Mercedes-Benz (Irvine), Mitsubishi (Cypress), Nissan (La Jolla), Porsche (Huntington Beach), Toyota (Newport Beach) and Volvo (Camarillo) have design centers in southern California, where there also are many independent design houses, such as Prisma Design (Tustin), established in 1997 by Gerhard Steinle.

Steinle had been senior vice president of design for Daimler-Benz and was sent to southern California in 1990 to establish the company's first design facility outside Germany. A few years later, he was called back to Germany, where he would have been the leading candidate to replace retiring Bruno Sacco as head of all Mercedes-Benz design.

But Steinle balked, because he and his family were so happy living in southern California. They decided to stay, and he opened his own studio.

"This is the dirty little secret of design," J Mays, Ford's vice president of design, says as he assumes a conspiratorial posture and almost whispers across the table:

"The West Coast studios aren't there because California is the center of the car culture. The West Coast studios are there because that's where designers want to live, and in order to get designers to come to work for you, you need to have a studio out there."

For example, Mays offers "my good buddy" Freeman Thomas, with whom Mays worked at the Simi Valley studio (former home of the VW/Audi studio) where they designed the Concept 1, the concept that became Volkswagen's New Beetle. Thomas eventually left VW/Audi to join Chrysler, which meant doing some time in Detroit before he took over DaimlerChryslser's Pacifica studio in Carlsbad, just north of San Diego.

"Now he's back in California and he's happy as a clam," Mays says, "and I'd be lying to you if I told you I don't miss it."

JERRY HIRSHBERG

Some concept cars are created to prepare the car-buying public for the shape of production cars that will be in dealer showrooms in a year or two. Other concepts provide the packaging to showcase new powertrains or innovative technology. Some concepts are little more than designer whimsy, exploring new shapes, alternative architectures and even entirely different modes of transportation.

But there's another, and very important reason, why concept cars are created.

"My target audience was our own corporation, a large bureaucratic entity that needed visual motivation to move forward, " says Jerry Hirshberg, who was lured away from General Motors in 1980 to establish Nissan's first design center outside of Japan.

Hirshberg's goal for concept vehicles was to show the corporation its own soul. He tried first with a vehicle called the Gobi, and later had stunning success with a car known simply as the Z.

Hirshberg studied at the Cleveland Institute of Art, and was fortunate that General Motors design chief Chuck Jordan experimented in the early 1960s by hiring graduates from places other than the traditional automotive design schools. Hirshberg rose quickly as a design manager at GM and was in charge of the Buick studio when he was recruited to establish a facility for Nissan.

Like Jordan, Nissan president Takashi Ishihara wanted to experiment, mixing what he considered to be intuitive Western designers with his company's agile engineers. Nissan considered sites and potential staff leaders in Europe and North America, and finally hired Hirshberg to establish Nissan Design International in La Jolla, California, just north of San Diego.

While doing car design as a profession, Hirshberg had a professor's fascination with the creative process.

"The worst thing you can do to creative people is to say you want them to be creative and 'we don't care how you do it'," Hirshberg notes. "Creativity begins when you have an obstacle or a challenge or new technology. It begins with narrowing your focus.

"What happens too often [with concept cars] is what I call automotive pornography. It's shockingly uncreative and largely unimaginative. When you take all the real-world limitations way from designers and creative people, you fall back on simply massaging exotic and exaggerated forms, and it's remarkable how similar they are over the years. They become remarkably familiar looking… Mistaking far-outness for extreme creativity is one of the biggest mistakes."

Soon after his retirement he published *The Creative Priority*, a book written to encourage, perhaps even to show corporations how to become "a fertile

ground — rather than a burial ground — for nourishing and growing innovative ideas." At least that's the way Hirshberg thinks it should be, although that wasn't always his own experience.

He recalls a meeting in which he represented design in a gathering at Los Angeles of Nissan engineers, marketing specialists, product planners and sales executives from Japan and the United States. The others in the room made it clear that while expensive cars might benefit from distinctive design, entry-level vehicles must have generic styling.

"Each discipline and culture brought its own viewpoints and priorities to the table. The engineers tended to think of design as something added to a product. Less of it, surely, would reduce the cost of an entry-level vehicle. The marketers and planners at the time thought of design as existing in stratified levels, consistent with the way they'd conceptualized the market, with the undifferentiated masses at the bottom ascending up through the ranks to the highly differentiated elite at the top. Hence, such needlessly pricey and trivial concepts as 'designer' jeans, home, and cars. And the Japanese, with their even more stratified society, had traditionally equated inexpensive, mass-market products with ordinary, commonplace design. To the designer, who perhaps naïvely believes every product has its own inherent truth, some soul to be expressed, these are confining, even threatening words."

One of Hirshberg's goals for concept vehicles is "to say this is what we can do if we were unhampered."

But, he adds, "creativity isn't an escape from disciplined thinking; it's an escape with disciplined thinking."

As he was driving back to San Diego from that meeting in Los Angeles, three objects caught Hirshberg's creatively disciplined and now emotionally charged eye: a grasshopper, a Bell helicopter and a truck, which, he notes, was, at that time, the "most humble,

Concept cars in a corporate context

108 Jerry Hirshberg began his design career at General Motors, but in 1980 was recruited away to establish Nissan's North American design center just north of San Diego, California.

109 While driving back to the studio after a disappointing corporate meeting in Los Angeles, Hirshberg pulled off the road and made these preliminary sketches for a revolutionary new concept vehicle, the Gobi (above).

generic and 'dumbed-down' of all entry-level vehicles.

"All at once, the three images coalesced, and a vision of a truck unlike any I'd ever seen assembled itself. It was as if a sports car had been rear-ended by a careening, loose truck bed, the two gracelessly jammed together and looking for all the world like some kind of helicopter on wheels. I pulled off Route 405 at the next exit and crudely sketched the image on a legal pad before it evaporated from my mind."

Back in the studio, Hirshberg reported to his designers, model-makers and engineers about the meeting, about his anger at what was said, and he showed them the sketch he'd drawn in the car. They shared his motivation and, working on their own, and

in secret, they spent two months creating a one-fourth scale model of what Hirshberg calls "a helicopter-like, grasshoppery truck," which they named Gobi. He carried that model with him to another meeting in Los Angeles.

"It was greeted with a chorus of surprised smiles and even applause. The president of Nissan at the time, Yukata Kume, a particularly bold, dynamic, and imaginative leader, happened to be present, and gave us the go-ahead to build a one-off running version — a roughly one-million-dollar commitment. He also instructed the marketing group to clinic the vehicle's potential as an addition to the lineup. All this from a project that had not been assigned."

But such can be the power of a concept car. "Concept cars," says Hirshberg, "should be three-dimensional questions that ask what if?"

The Gobi, which was the first concept car done by Nissan's North American studio, certainly asked that question, and it asked it for quite a while. While most concept cars have a very brief shelf life, Gobi, introduced at the North American International Auto Show in Detroit in 1999, spent several years on the international auto show circuit. Its boldly juxtaposed design elements somehow worked well together and the concept won numerous awards and was featured in a documentary movie. But, in the end, one American business magazine simply labeled the Gobi as "finest unbuilt vehicle in the world." Nissan's own financial woes, trade issues between the U.S. and Japan and the vehicle's own extreme design combined to prevent Gobi from moving from the auto show stand to dealership showrooms. The Gobi might have been the small, practical utility vehicle that could have convinced Americans that size isn't everything and at the same time might have enabled Europeans to understand why Americans are so strongly attached to their trucks and sport utility vehicles.

"Asked at the end of my career if there was one vehicle I regretted never quite made it to the road, without question it was the Gobi," says Hirshberg. "Ironically, in the atmosphere of today's Nissan, with Carlos Ghosn at the helm, there's no question it would have made it." Ironically, at the time Nissan was turning its back on what might have been a breakthrough vehicle in a category, small trucks, that Nissan had introduced in North American in 1953 with its Datsun model.

Nissan's financial woes worsened and in 1999 it entered into partnership with Renault. The French automaker installed Carlos Ghosn, a native of Brazil who had been a highly effective executive, first at Michelin and then for Renault, as Nissan's president. Ghosn established a revitalization plan and Nissan's corporate comeback has been remarkable. But while Ghosn's leadership may have been the key, the success of Nissan's vehicle sales also is the result of very strong styling under Shiro Nakamura, an Art Center graduate

and former General Motors designer who was hired in 1999 to lead Nissan design.

"While disappointed the car was never released for sale, we were nonetheless gratified that the project introduced the language of design into the corporate strategy dialogue," Hirshberg wrote. "It had a profound impact on the way Nissan (and other corporations) thought about trucks, entry-level vehicles, design, and the market."

Gobi also had revealed to Nissan a part of its own soul. Hirshberg says that one of the "least common" reasons to do a concept is car "when someone literally has a spark," which he explains is an idea that doesn't fit, for which there isn't room in the corporate portfolio, but which captures the corporate soul and thus needs to be nurtured.

"Gobi was like that," he says, "More recently there was the Z concept car. It was just a passion of mine, frankly, when nobody was talking about the Z and the corporation was in peril and badly in debt. I held a meeting and said, 'If any one of you were running the corporation, what would be the one thing you would do right now?'" Various designers and others working at Nissan's La Jolla outpost offered their opinions. Finally, it was Hirshberg's turn.

"When it came to me, I said I'd bring back the Z."

If any vehicle ever had displayed Nissan's soul, it was the 240Z. Introduced as a 1970 model, the Z was a light, nimble, fast and affordable. It had the styling of an exotic European sports car, the mechanical efficiency and practical technology that made Japanese cars so attractive, and it was brought to market — and at an affordable price — by Yutuka Katayama, the legendary "Mr. K." who for many years was manager of Nissan's American sales arm. But over time, the Z car grew larger, heavier and much more expensive. In many ways, the story of the Z car was the story of corporate bureaucracy and of Nissan itself. Hirshberg realized that relationship, and he proposed the rebirth of the Z, which ended production in 1996, but "the reaction of the corporation was that we needed bread and butter cars, not toys," he recalls.

"There was a lot of resistance, so I used a concept car

110-111 While Ajay Panchal worked on his sketches, Jerry Hirshberg and Nissan's North American public relations director Jason Vines found a way to fund construction of a Z car concept. The rebirth of the 350Z marked more than the return of a famous sports car; it provided tangible evidence of the renewal of Nissan's corporate spirit.

platform and worked with the public relations department," Hirshberg says of his co-conspirator, Nissan's North American p.r. director Jason Vines, who found a way to fund the construction of a Z concept car.

"We were an outlaw duo," Hirshberg admits. "The purpose was to corner the corporation into building the car. I believed that if we got it out there [as a concept], there would be a campaign [of public support] to build it, and that's exactly what happened."

The Nissan Z Concept made its debut in January 1999 at Detroit. Hirshberg was right. There was an immediate demand from car enthusiasts for Nissan to put a new Z car into production (and it certainly didn't hurt that Ghosn had driven a Z car when he worked at Michelin, and had fond memories of the experience). At Detroit, Vines told *AutoWeek* magazine that anticipation of a possible return of the Z "has given a lot of people

at Nissan a reason to live again." And Nissan's still very secret corporate approval of the project also gave those people time to carefully think about what the new Z should be. The Z Concept was almost too retro in its design. Hirshberg recognized that the car needed to be what he calls "referential," something that "would have an immediate connection with the Z even if we didn't put the letter on it." He wanted it to evoke the historic Z cars, but not to be a virtual reproduction as he was seeing done by other some automakers.

"The first [concept] car opened a dialogue — a very interesting in-house dialogue — of going retro or not," says Ajay Panchal, exploratory designer at what now is known as Nissan Design America. Although "I wasn't even born when the first Z was launched," Panchal, born in Britain of parents from India, became the lead designer for the reborn Z car.

"We really fought hard to go against that [retro] grain," says Panchal. "Both the 240 and the 300Z were iconic for the generations they represented. But I did not use their design cues too literally. I picked more subtle cues. I liked the scooped, hollow headlights [on the original 240Z] and started with that, but stretched it [so] the whole body side is concave."

Panchal is proud of the Z's design details and that the car's lack of gimmicky hardware are true to the car's original heritage. For example, he notes that one of the first things he did was the door handle, which often is an afterthought, but in the case of the 350Z helped set a pattern for other details. After showing the original Z Concept at Detroit in 1999, Nissan returned in 2001 with an updated Z concept that actually was a mildly camouflaged precursor to the production 350Z unveiled later that year at the Tokyo show.

While the original Z Concept was retro, this new one was a modern car, but one that nonetheless immediately and clearly displayed its heritage, and Nissan's recaptured soul.

CULTURE SHOCK

112 top The Toyota POD concept vehicle features drive-by-wire technology. Its driver uses a joystick-style controller for steering, acceleration and braking.

112 center POD's interior design theme is the circle, symbol of family unity. Each seat has its own monitor that welcomes occupants with a smiling character. The monitor on the dashboard displays images to encourage safe driving.

112-113 bottom POD's occupants aren't alone in receiving emotional signals. The car's face uses colors to express a range of 10 emotions, such as angry (red) when the driver has to slam on the brakes or sad (dark blue) when the car runs out of fuel.

T he Tokyo Motor Show is held biennially, and some would say that it is fitting that this auto show is staged in odd-numbered years.

That's because Tokyo showcases some of the oddest concept cars ever created. Consider the Daihatsu D-Bag 4, the Suzuki Wagon R/LoFT, Mitsubishi's Maus and Zaus, the Toyota Will Vi, the Nissan Nails, the Mazda Secret Hideout and the Isuzu Begin Funkybox, and those are just a few of the recent Tokyo concepts that have odd names. Where things get really weird is not with the names of some of the concept vehicles shown at Tokyo, but with their nature.

Consider the Honda Unibox, a six-wheeled, six-seat vehicle with see through body panels. Included inside the Unibox are two, small electric motorcycles, a shopping cart with its own navigation system (so you don't miss any sales?), while mounted on the front of the 'box' is an exterior airbag (to protect pedestri-

ans should your attention wander as you wander around the city, looking for a parking place?).

Or consider the Toyota POD. POD stands for "Personalized On Demand." That personalization includes monitoring the driver's pulse and perspiration levels, using music and cool air to try to relax a tense driver, and even warning those in other cars of the driver's mood through toots on the horn, wags of its tail-like antenna and by the car's "face."

With the rear-view mirrors serving as ears, the headlights as eyes and with light-emitting diodes (LEDs) in the shape of a nose and mouth, POD also uses color to express up to 10 emotions, including happy, sleepy, sad and angry.

But special mention must be made of the Honda Fuya-jo, because it qualifies in both categories of strangeness. Fuya-jo is Japanese for "the castle that never sleeps." But this vehicle's nature is even stranger than its name. Fuya-jo looks like a tall, raspberry-colored toaster on wheels, and is an automotive tribute to Japan's youthful dance club culture.

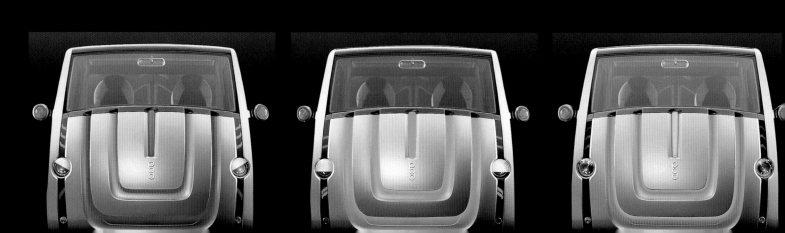

Thinking outside the box at the Tokyo show

Fuya-jo is sort of a boom box on wheels, with a turntable-like steering wheel and with "seats" that have the occupants all but standing, so they can dance their way down the road.

Dance slowly, that is; Fuya-jo's 1.0-liter engine propels it to a top speed of only 19 miles per hour. But, notes Bryon Fitzpatrick, a native of Australia who designed cars in Europe before becoming a design educator in America, "they are the most exciting cars at the moment. They're totally out of the box, so to speak, except that some of them look like boxes. It's the most exciting stuff we've seen in the last couple of years and it's so far away from the conservative approach of Toyota and Honda [production vehicles]. It's astonishing to see the Tokyo auto show."

And, Fitzpatrick adds, "When they [the Japanese] party, they do it hard. The cars could be a version of that."

Iwao Koizumi, a chief designer at Mazda, isn't comfortable with that party-hardy image. He explains that for the Japanese automakers, the Tokyo show is like a *matsuri*, a festival.

"Usually," Koizumi says, "Japanese people live their ordinary, everyday lives without expressing their emotions." But, when it is time for a festival, they are free to "express their positive emotions."

"The Tokyo Motor Show is a very good opportunity for the Japanese makers to express the emotion that is kept in in everyday life," he adds. "The show cars stand out from everyday living. That's the main reason why many Japanese show cars are totally different from production cars."

"Not only is the Tokyo show a festival, but it also has a theme, 'meeting the environmental challenge or whatever,'" says Tsutomu "Tom" Matano, who designed cars for General Motors, Volvo, BMW and Mazda before becoming director of industrial design at the Academy of Art College in San Francisco. "Given this theme, the companies come up answers."

In the case of concept cars, those answers can be as unusual as the wording of the themes themselves.

For example, the theme at Tokyo for 2001, when Toyota presented POD and Honda its Unibox, was

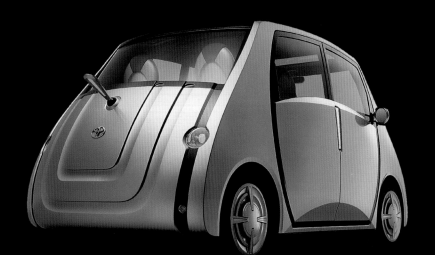

113 top POD's seats swivel and have built-in speakers and vibration transducers so occupants can feel the music as well as hear it.

113 bottom right POD, which was jointly developed by Toyota and Sony, shares its range of emotions with traffic behind by wagging its antenna tail.

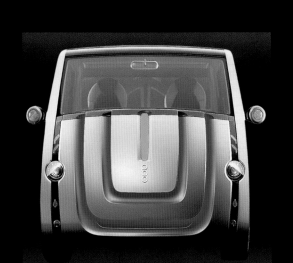

"Open the door! The Automobile's Bright Future."

In 1999, the theme was "Eye to the Future. Changing Vehicles for the Earth." Honda responded with Fuya-jo and Ford's J Mays hired Marc Newson, whose furniture and other designs are considered prized works of modern art, to do his first automobile, the Ford 021C. Consider this explanation of the 1997 theme — "One World. One People. One Show":

We wish to create, together with our close companions, lives with cars loaded with our modest happiness, by which we can each express our own personalities.

Together with loved ones, families and friends we can understand each other. The earth demands that we treasure our lives together, and the environment, and cleverly use its limited resources, with loving care by each individual. The world motoring society has become one, for manufacturers and users to get together to make our lives with vehicles better than ever.

The Tokyo Motor Show is the rendezvous plaza for vehicles and people to get together.

To think together about the car life of the future. One World. One People. One Show.

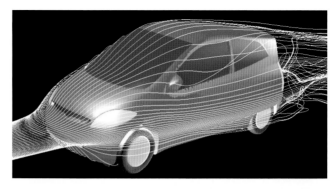

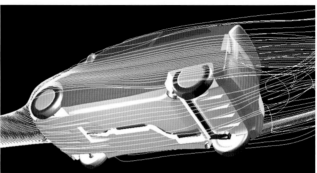

114 left and bottom right The Daihatsu U4B takes its name from its design theme: an Urban 4x4 Buggy. Although compact at 3395 mm (133.7 inches), the U4B has room for four adults.

114 top right UFE is a Daihatsu concept for Ultra Fuel Economy that made its debut at the Tokyo show in 2001. A plastic composite body and the use of aluminum components allow it to weigh in at 603 kilograms (less than 1,400 pounds).

While companies in other cultures might ignore an auto show or festival's theme — for example, consider these far-beyond modest theme busters presented at Tokyo in 1997: BMW's Z07, Mercedes-Benz massive Maybach, Volkswagen's W12 supercar and Cadillac's right-hand-drive Seville — that doesn't happen in Japan. "We do specific cars for the Tokyo

114 center right The car's fuel efficiency is enhanced by its aerodynamic design with a cut tail at the back of its teardrop silhouette. The streamlined theme carries over into the interior, which features a winged instrument panel.

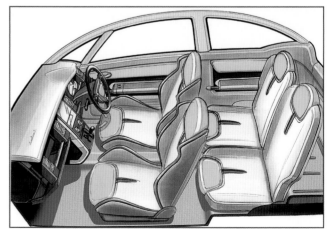

115 center The Daihatsu FF Ultra Space uses a low floor, sliding rear doors and a large sunroof to create a bright, open and easily accessible interior.

115 bottom So rear-seat passengers can watch movies as they travel, video monitors are built into the backs of the FF Ultra Spaces's front seats.

115 top Daihatsu named this trapezoidal concept Muse because of its "Magic use." The car was presented at Tokyo in 2001 as a small car of high quality. Its features include a 10.4-inch liquid crystal display panel that can provide everything from news and weather reports to fortune-telling services.

show," Matano says. Nissan concept designer Ajay Panchal notes that his company builds a half dozen or more concept cars for the Tokyo show and at least one of them is what he calls "totally blue sky, an idea factory" that has no basis in potential series production. "The point," he says, "is to show a spirit, a personality and to communicate to a specific audience, such as an audience that would want to dance inside a vehicle as it cruised between nightclubs."

"If that car came to the shows in the United States," he adds, "you'd miss the context."

And context is crucial in understanding the Japanese cars — concepts or production vehicles — says Matano. To explain why concepts can be so wacky while production cars so conservative, Matano expands on his comments about giving answers, which means something very different in Japan than it does in Western cultures.

"In the Japanese educational system," he explains,

"students are taught to respond with the right answer. It's not so much the process as the answer," he adds, noting that while American students may get credit, for example, for using the right formulas while missing the specific answer, in Japan the grade is strictly for achieving the right answer. "In Japan," Matano says, "it's the right answer or the wrong answer, and if it's the wrong answer, you're out. That's the only explanation I can give for why the Japanese [production cars] look so much alike. They come to the same answer."

That may explain why, as former Isuzu and

Mazda designer Peter Montero notes, "when you have a chance to do a concept vehicle [for Tokyo], you have all this pent-up creativity. You go hog wild and do everything you would never to able to do [in a production vehicle]." Montero, who designs for JCI, a major automotive supplier, lived for several years in Japan. "On one hand you have a very conservative, very performance-oriented culture and on the other hand you have the inevitable reaction to that in the form of wild outposts within that culture."

"I think there is a strong movement in Japan to come up with designs that appeal to the young gen-

eration," says Wu-Huang Chin, a Chinese-born American designer for Mazda. "I wouldn't claim that I understand the young people in Japan, but they seem to really like alternative design, things that are not mainstream."

"People have two sides," notes Japan-native Ken Okuyama, who worked for Porsche, General Motors and Pininfarina before accepting the chairmanship of the transportation design department at the Art Center College of Design in Pasadena, California. While the Japanese automakers may have become conservative in production design, "at the same time, to show the creativity of designers and of engineers, they use concept cars as a tool," he says, "and sometimes they use them to change the image of the company, not necessarily where they will be, but where they want to be."

"I think culturally the car represents something different to the Japanese than it does to Americans," says Dan Sims, an American who is design director at Mitsubishi Design America, the Japanese automaker's styling studio in southern California.

"Here, all of us have childhood memories of cars, and they've become an inherent part of our DNA. There are a lot of unspoken things about cars that we appreciate here.

"But if you look at the situation in Japan, the automobile was a rare commodity prior to the war.

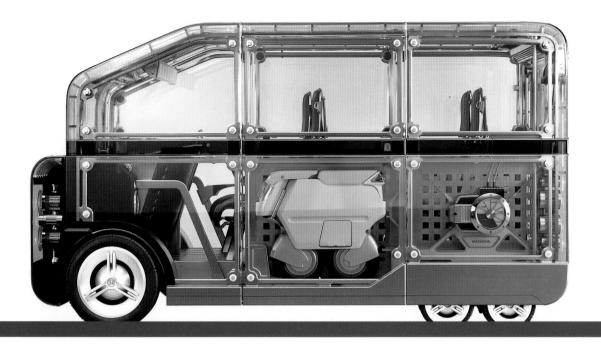

117 top The Honda Unibox rides on six wheels, but riding inside are a pair of electric motorcycles and a shopping cart complete with its own navigation system (perhaps so you can find your way back to the Unibox after a long day of shopping). The Unibox provides seating for six people, and a front-mounted airbag to protect pedestrians who might wander into its path.

116 Toyota's DMT (Dual Mode Traveler) features unusual architecture that has its two passengers seated so high above the pavement that they need steps to descend into the vehicle's large cargo area. The DMT's versatility includes a center cluster that can slide from side to side along the vehicle's dashboard.

117 bottom The WiLL VC is a "cybercapsule" designed to provide the latest in network telematic services through Toyota's G-Book access to information and entertainment. WiLL is a joint venture between Toyota and six other companies that united to appeal to innovation-hungry young customers. In addition to a line of vehicles, the WiLL label can be found on household appliances and even beverages, all targeted at a youthful, hip part of the Japanese marketplace.

A lot of companies, Mitsubishi included, made cars, even in the 1930s, but it was more of an experiment on the part of heavy industries rather than making cars for the public.

"So, for the most part," he continues, "cars had to be imported and they were very, very expensive. After the war, Japan began to rebuild. It wasn't until into the '50s when Toyota and Nissan were making cars on a mass-produced scale.

"A lot of people in Japan today, when they grew up there wasn't a car at home. In fact, in some places, like Tokyo, you can probably survive better without a car. With tolls and parking, a car represents something different. It represents a luxury, a status. But it's evolving. To the older post-war generation, like our baby boomers, it's a status symbol and they like a car to represent status. But the young people say, 'that's with our parents, we're into cars as a functional tool.'

"That's where you're getting all the 'box' cars that look like something from the designers at Steelcase [an office furniture maker], trying to get the maximum space on the minimum footprint. That's what drives the wackiness."

"In Tokyo," adds designer turned educator Tom Matano, "some of the concept cars aren't based on the automobile as popular transportation. In Japan, you don't necessarily need the car as everyday transportation. The concepts tend to deviate from carrying things or people to become something else, a boom box or whatever, not necessarily a mode for transportation.

"Some of the concepts just don't make sense if you look at them as day-to-day vehicles, but in Japan, they do make sense."

118-119 Japanese automakers aren't the only ones who present extremely exotic vehicles on the floor of the Tokyo show. Volkswagen unveiled its W12 Synchro concept at Tokyo in 1997 and returned in 2001 with the W12 World Record. The scissor-doored VW concept was designed by Italdesign-Giugiaro and carries a 600-horsepower 12-cylinder engine. A special Nardo version of the concept averaged more than 200 miles per hour (322.891 km/h) in an endurance test.

120-121 and 121 right
In the mid-1980s, Subaru's
lineup included a couple of
small, boxy cars, a mundane
compact sedan and the
angular Alcyone/XT coupe.
But at the Tokyo show in
1985 the automotive arm of
Fuji Heavy Industries broke
out of its mold. The F-9X
concept had lines that were
long and curved. The F-9X
concept carried a
turbocharged 2.0-liter flat-
four engine to provide power
to its four-wheel-drive chassis.
In 1991, Subaru introduced
its new production sports
coupe, the SVX, designed by
Giugiaro at Italdesign. The
SVX made a strong styling
statement because of its
window-in-window design —
very large side windows but
with only a small lower
portion that opened.

120 bottom Mercedes-Benz used the Tokyo show in 1997 as the stage for the return — in the form of a concept car — of the Maybach, a famous marque that produced custom-built cars in the 1920s and '30s. Wilhelm Maybach designed Gottlieb Daimler's first Mercedes car. Later he and his son Karl built their own cars. The Maybach concept was a dream car designed around an owner who would ride in the back seat, with access to a 20-inch flat-screen television, humidor, assorted beverages and a fully reclining seat, while the chauffeur handled the driving.

121 bottom BMW designed the Z07 to show how its famed 507 of the 1950s might look had it continued in production. The Z07 was the first BMW concept done by the company's own design department. It made its debut at the Tokyo show in 1997. The Z07 is a roadster concept and has no soft convertible top. However, it can be equipped with a tonneau cover that includes the large faring behind the driver's head or with a removable hard top that protects the driver and passenger from inclement weather.

DRIVING, ITALIAN

T he Buick Y-Job wasn't the only significant birth in 1938. Nearly half a world away, in a small country far from the United States, three other births were taking place as Harley Earl and his team at General Motors' Art and Color Section were midwifing what is recognized as the world's first true dream car.

The country was Italy. The babies were Leonardo Fioravanti, Marcello Gandini and Giorgetto Giugiaro, each of whom would grow up to have a profound influence on the design of both concept cars and production vehicles driven by customers around the world.

"We are as a country not so rich, not so important worldwide, but we are the fourth largest [automotive] market worldwide," says Leonardo Fioravanti. "Why? Because Italians love cars."

Italians also love to design cars, and the world loves to drive those cars, or at least to dream of driving those cars.

With his right hand, Leonardo Fioravanti drew the design concepts for eight Ferraris.

Marcello Gandini's credits include the Lamborghini Countach, the car that rivaled *Charlie's Angel* Farrah Fawcett for the place of honor on the wall of seemingly every teenage boy on the planet in the 1970s.

Giorgetto Giugiaro's list of vehicles is so long — so many cars for so many manufacturers — that a panel of international automotive journalists voted him the most influential car designer of the entire twentieth century.

Fioravanti. Gandini. Giugiaro. Sons whose work would make any mother proud. Yet Italy begat these legends of automotive design in a single year, and in the years before and since she has produced their many fathers, sons and brothers who helped make Italy even more important in automotive design than it is in the world of fashion.

Paolo Caccamo, chief executive of I.DE.A, suggests that it is no coincidence that the northern Italian cities of Milan and Turin are the fashion capitals of the world. Milano is the house of couture. Torino is home to Bertone and to Pininfarina and to Italdesign and to I.DE.A and has been home to so many others that have driven Italian style from the narrow streets that run between the city's arcaded sidewalks to the highways of the world.

STYLE

122 The Aria was a roadster concept done by I.DE.A., the Italian design and engineering firm, for the automaking arm of India's Tata Group. Aria made its debut at Geneva in 2000.

123 top left Vuscia was a 1996 concept car from I.DE.A. that put a stylish yet roomy "unispace" multi-purpose vehicle body around components from a Fiat Brava. Vuscia was unveiled at the Turin show in 1996.

123 top right I.DE.A. designed a coupe concept, based on the Aria roadster, for the New Delhi auto show in 2000. The production version of the Tata Aria was unveiled early in 2001 at Geneva.

123 center, bottom left and bottom right The Keio University Advanced Zero-Emission Vehicle has eight wheels and seats for eight passengers and established an electric-vehicle speed record of 311 kilometers/hour (more than 192 miles per hour) in testing.

124 and 125 Italdesign
presented its Bugatti EB112
concept in 1993. After
Volkswagen won control of
the famous marque in 1998,
it commissioned new
concepts built around VW's
W18 engine. A full-size
model of a coupe was built
(left), but when the Bugatti
EB218 made its auto show
debut, at Geneva in 1999, it
was as a spectacular sedan.

But those designers have not driven alone. They have worked with Turin's skilled craftsmen and with its engineering community and technology experts to maintain the city's position as the driving force of automotive design.

"As a native of Turin, I would like to say that we Turinese are famous for inventing things and then losing them," says Roberto Piatti, managing director of Stile Bertone. Piatti notes that Turin was the home of Italian cinema, until it moved to Rome, and was the home of Italian fashion, until that industry moved to Milan.

"Fortunately," he adds, "this did not happen with car design, "Turin enters the third millennium with a group of operators in the automotive sector who are varied in size and specialization, but as a collective force are difficult to find elsewhere. Turin is one of the few places in the world where it is still possible to develop a new vehicle from the blank piece of paper to production.

"These are services which every major European, American, Japanese or Korean automobile manufacturer can find at home, but often they come to Turin to find stimulation and alternatives to the creativity of their internal design centers, or because the development of the engineering phase or the construction of a certain prototype in Turin can offer advantages in terms of both time and money when compared to similar activities supplied by internal departments."

Because of its reputation for automotive design, the city also attracts a stream of young designers from other nations and from other cultures.

They come not necessarily for formal education — often they already have completed studies at one of the well-known design schools in the United States or England — but they come to Turin for something the schools may not teach, says Sergio Pininfarina. "Designers go to school to learn the technique, to learn the technology," says Pininfarina. "I contend that in the schools of design you can teach the way of design, but not what to design. What to design is in your blood, is in your brain, and is very, very difficult to teach. This is something the painters, the artists have in their mind, in their blood. There is no school for that. The best education is to see and to work

together. Young people come to us because they think that to spend a few months or a few years at Pininfarina is worthwhile to their careers. Some stay, some go away and I find many of my 'sons' working in Japan, in France, in Germany."

One of Sergio's many "sons" is Ken Okuyama, who interrupted his career at General Motors just so he could work for the famed Italian design house. "Pininfarinas have been my dream cars since childhood," says Okuyama, who was born in Japan and studied automotive design in California. "It's not just the Ferraris they did, but also the cars they designed for Peugeot and Alfa Romeo and Honda. I worked for General Motors for 10 years and finally said to myself, 'this will be my last chance in life to work for Pininfarina'." So Okuyama left GM in the mid-1990s and moved to Italy, where he worked for 5 1/2 years and helped design the Rossa concept car as well as the Ferrari production model that bears the

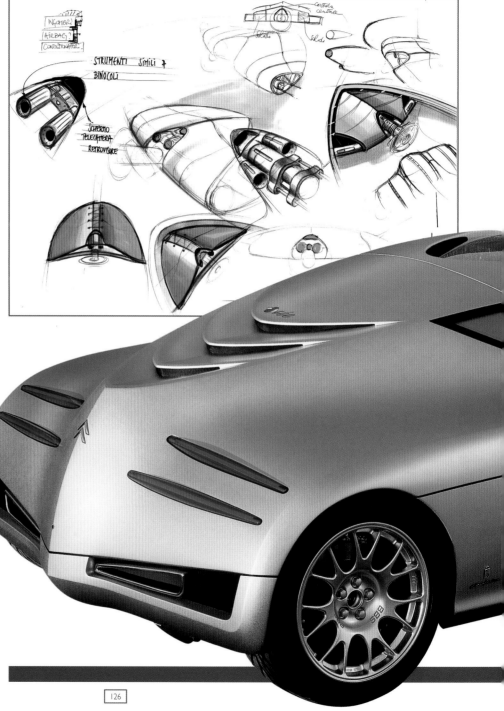

name of the company's founder, the Enzo Ferrari.

After his stay at Pininfarina, Okuyama returned to America as chairman of transportation design at the Art Center College of Design in Pasadena.

While the young designers learn first-hand from what Piatti calls "the grand masters of Turin," Turin also benefits, he says, by refueling its own creativity, enhancing the strength in its own traditions with a continual exchange of ideas — and challenges — not only with young designers but with corporate clients from around the world. However, the core values remain and thus Turin can "go against the flow if necessary."

Or, as Leonardo Fioravanti phases it: "Italians are always Italians."

When designing a concept car, "you want something that's unique and distinctive and cutting edge and breaking new ground," says David Stollery, an American auto designer who worked as a freelancer in Italy before joining the General Motors design department and later launching Toyota's North American studio. "But at the same time it has to be appropriate and

attractive to people, something that is good looking," Stollery adds. "That's something the Italians always did."

Indeed. All you need to do is to look at the recent concepts from any of the Italian studios. Bertone opened the 1990s with its emotionally appealing Chevrolet Corvette Nivola, and in 1992 produced both its sensational Blitz and its tiny Fiat Cinquecento Rush roadster. Soon to follow was its gull-winged Porsche-based Karima, "off-road" coupes based on Fiat and Opel mechanicals, a BMW-based vehicle that combined the best aspects of both a speedster and a pickup truck. Soon after the turn of the century it changed vehicle interior architecture with its Filo and Novanta drive-by-wire concepts.

Meanwhile, Pininfarina was doing its Mythos, Chronos, Nautilus, Rossa and Citroën-based Osee exotics as well as an interesting series of small cars, including the Eta Beta, Wish, Metrocube and a succession of Ethos vehicles.

At Italdesign, the Giugiaros looked at opposite sides of the van equation in 1992 with the tiny Biga and the gigantic Columbus. Giugiaro has always enjoyed the exploration of alternative and versatile vehicle architecture and presented such concepts as Machimoto, Lucciola, the Formula 4 and Formula Hammer, Structura, but it also did more than its share of exotic supercars with such concepts as the Lamborghini Cala, Bugatti EB series, Maserati Buron and Kubang, the Volkswagen W12 and the Alfa Romeo Scighera and Brera.

Turin's "Big Four" are Bertone, Pininfarina, Italdesign and I.DE.A. Each can take a concept car from its first sketch — now made on a computer screen, not on a drawing table — through its various and detailed stages of development, working internal-

128 In 2000, Pininfarina showed its StreetKa concept, a roadster based on Ford's Ka. A few months later, an agreement was signed to begin production of a new Ford model based on the Pininfarina design. Perhaps as a way to celebrate, Pininfarina unveiled the Ka-based Start coupe at Frankfurt in 2001.

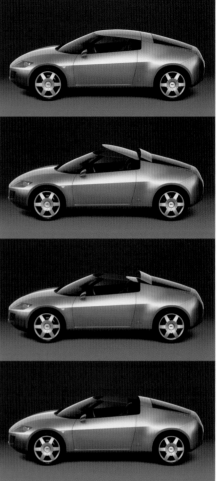

129 top left and right Start starts out as a 2+2 coupe, and one powered by a four-cylinder engine turbocharged to more than 200 horsepower. But at the touch of a button, the top retracts to turn Start into an open-air sports car.

129 center, bottom left and bottom right Start's interior uses exposed steel tubes in the door and center tunnel to evoke the roll cage that protects occupants in race and rally cars, but hand-stitched leather on the seats and dashboard add a rich elegance.

ly or with other experts in Turin to produce a finished vehicle for display at an international auto show, or even one ready for series production on the client's assembly line. Bertone and Pininfarina have their own production facilities and produce series of limited-edition vehicles for their international automaker clients.

"From all over the world they come to Torino to have the prototypes made, the concept cars made," says Sergio Pininfarina, who adds that even when they design their concept cars in their own studios — in America, Asia or elsewhere Europe — manu-facturers still come to Turin for styling consultation and to have those concepts built. "Because we have the technology and also the craftsmanship," he explains. And because the Italians have their passion.

"Italian design," Pininfarina continues, "expresses first the rich love for the product. The Italian view is something that is elegant, responsive to the joy of driving. It is strong, and very emotional."

"Why do we have our concepts built in Turin?" designer Gerry McGovern of Ford repeats the question, and then laughs aloud at his answer: "I love Italian food and culture!" Turning serious, the design director for Ford's Lincoln and Mercury brands says that he was mystified at first by the fact that it seemed to take quite a while for work to begin when he first went to coach builder Stola to have the Lincoln Mk. 9 concept built. "You get the impression that they don't know what the hell they're doing," he said, "but then suddenly the thing all comes together and you realize that they know what they're doing."

And well they should. "They have quite a heritage in terms of building show cars and prototypes,"

McGovern adds of Stola, a company that began building car bodies in 1919. But, McGovern adds, it's not just the level of coachbuilding competence and craftsmanship that he likes about having concepts built in Turin, "A lot of it has to do with personality, with building a relationship."

That relationship has become so strong, he adds, that he doubts that he'll ever look to other locations for concept car construction. In fact, he says, to complete the interior styling of a couple of recent concepts, he stationed a few of his own company's designers in Turin and also enlisted help from local designers.

Automakers continue to come to Turin for design expertise. Roberto Piatti remembers how a young Japanese auto industry sought the help of Italian designers. The Koreans have done the same thing, and now the budding auto industry in China and South America and other emerging markets comes for design and engineering solutions, to share in what Piatti calls "a mental flexibility and a freedom of expression which is unique in the world."

130-131 Pininfarina celebrated its 70th anniversary, and its long relationship with Ferrari, by unveiling the Rossa concept at Turin in 2000. The name recalls the famous Testa Rossa while the design seeks to balance solid masses and open spaces. Rossa has no top and only a thin windscreen that harkens to the early days of sports car racing. Pininfarina describes the cockpit as "no more than a driver-sized niche carved out of the car's flowing lines."

132-133 The Pininfarina Enjoy is both a roadster and a racer. The concept, which made its debut at Geneva in 2003, drew inspiration from motorcycles, both in its dynamics and in the way its mechanical parts serve as design features. Enjoy's most striking design features are its fenders, which can be removed to convert the sporty roadster into an open-wheel racer. Pininfarina worked with Lotus to make sure the concept's ride, handling and four-cylinder engine are truly enjoyable.

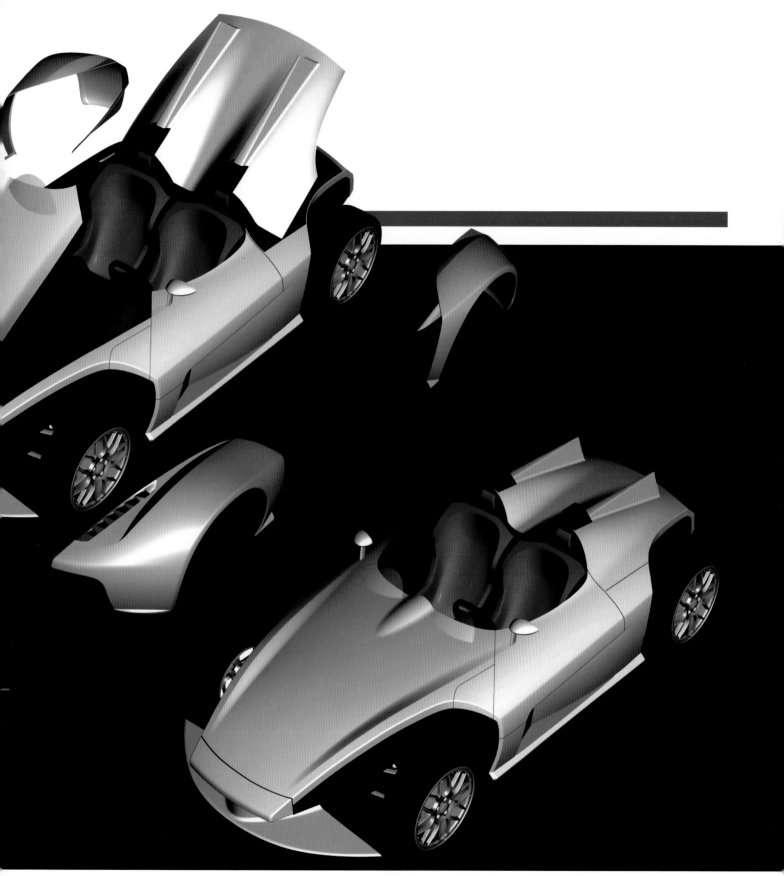

GIUGIARO

The risks and rewards of creativity

Giorgetto Giugiaro's artistic talent was obvious, and inherited. His grandfather, Luigi, was a painter of frescoes in churches and patrician homes in northwestern Italy. His father, Mario, also did frescoes, as well as painting with oils on canvas. Luigi and Mario taught young Giorgetto how to mix colors, how to create sculptural shading while working in only two dimensions, and how to exploit light and shadow and the nuances of surface. Giorgetto was barely a teenager when his father told him it was time to pursue a more formal education, one that would add a technical perspective to his inherent artistic talent. So, at the age of 14, Giorgetto Giugiaro moved to the big city, to Torino, to study art by day and technical drawing at night. An exhibit of student art, including Giugiaro's watercolors of automobiles, was visited by his instructor's nephew, Dante Giacosa, who as technical director of Fiat was responsible for the design and creation of the famed Topolino and many other cars. Giacosa saw such promise in the student's work that he offered Giugiaro an apprenticeship in the Fiat design studio. Before his 18th birthday, and while still attending school, Giugiaro was working full-time in Fiat's Special Vehicle Design Studies department.

134-135 Seen head on, Aspid may look much like any typical sports car concept designed in the late 1980s. How, you might wonder, could designer Giorgetto Giugiaro be considered the most influential designer of the entire century?

"I started as a young boy to do this work," Giugiaro says. "When I joined Fiat in 1965, I was 17." Giugiaro was only 21 when Nuccio Bertone saw some of his drawings. At an age when many auto designers are just starting their graduate studies in art school, Giugiaro found himself succeeding the legendary Franco Scaglione as head of styling for one of Italy's most famous *carrozzeria*. In addition to doing production car designs for Alfa Romeo, BMW, Iso Rivolta, Fiat and Mazda, Giugiaro designed such concepts as the Aston Martin DB4 GT Jet, the Maserati 5000 GT, the Ferrari 250 GT, the Alfa Romeo Canguro and Testudo, a concept which would have impact on future production designs from Porsche (the 928) and Mazda (the RX-7).

136 top and 137 It's been said that it looks as if Giugiaro carved the Aspid and his other 1988 concepts like a sculptor rather than drawing them like an artist. Aspid's engine is mounted behind the driver's and passenger's seats, with a large area for luggage or other cargo behind the engine.

136 bottom Asgard applies similar design themes to a minivan architecture and provides seating for eight people in what looks like a land-bound space capsule.

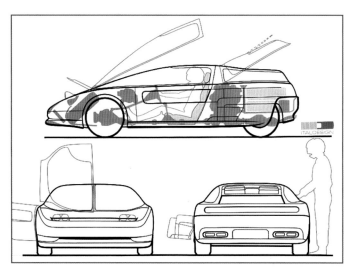

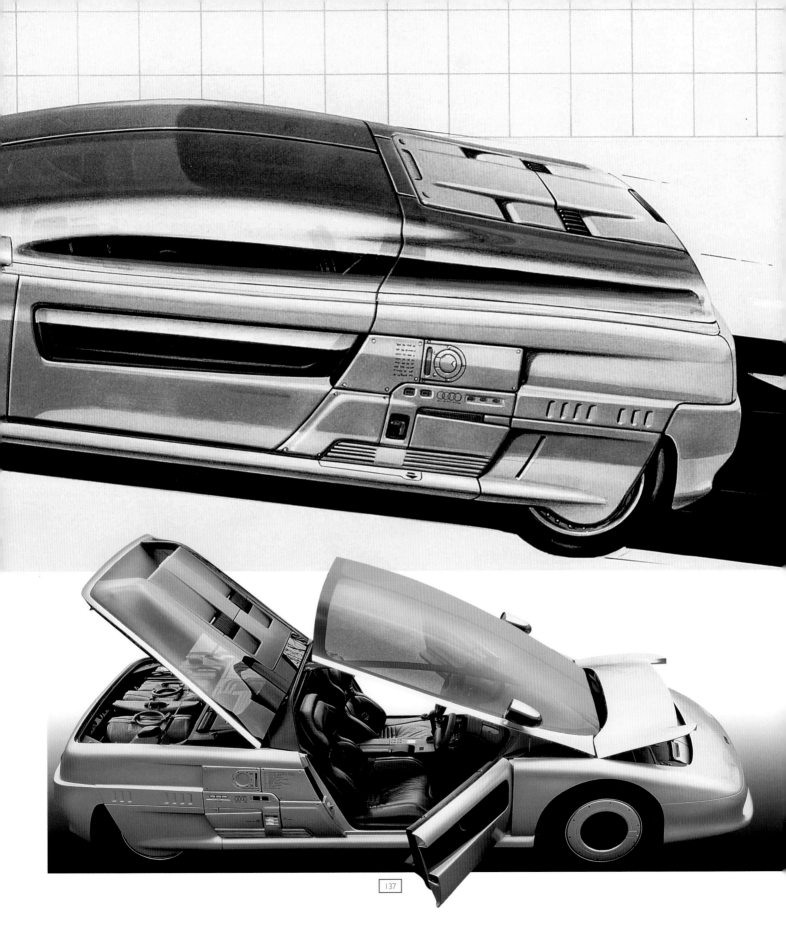

After nearly six years at Bertone, Giugiaro accepted another offer, to become manager with responsibility for design and prototype building at Ghia's Style and Projects Center. Within one year, Giugiaro had five concepts ready for international auto shows, including the Maserati Ghibli and the De Tomaso Mangusta sports cars, the electric-powered Rowan and the Fiat Vanessa, a car designed for women drivers and their children.

Giugiaro's time at Ghia was fertile, but it also was fleeting. He left when Alejandro De Tomaso took control of the company. Giugiaro established Ital Styling, an independent design studio, then soon united with former Fiat engineer Aldo Mantovani to establish an automotive design and prototype-building company that carried the official name of Italian Society for the Realization of Prototypes, or SIRP. The company was better known by its unofficial name, Ital Design, and later became Italdesign-Giugiaro, an international design and engineering company based in a Turin suburb where its buildings look like a pair of space stations that have landed on Earth. The company also has satellite studios in France and California.

138 top The most radical
of Giugiaro's 1988 trilogy of
concepts is Aztec, which
features a twin-cockpit
design with separate
windscreens that wrap
around the driver and
passenger, who are exposed
to the open air.

138-139 and 139
The access doors on the
side of Giugiaro's radical
1988 concepts house such
things as a hydraulic lift,
power outlet, air compressor,
fire extinguisher, oil-changing
system and a gauge that
monitors the air filter.

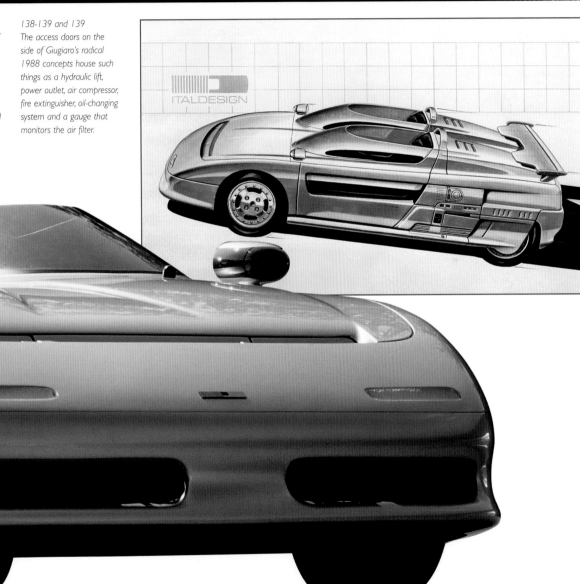

ITALDESIGN

140-141 The Bugatti EB112 made its debut in 1993 at the Geneva show. Volkswagen bought Bugatti in 1998 and had Giugiaro design additional Bugatti concepts, including the EB118 coupe and EB218 sedan, although now around VW's W18 engine instead of the EB112's V8.

140 bottom When the Bugatti marque was reborn, Giugiaro first designed a coupe concept, the Bugatti ID 90. Then, in 1993, he used styling cues from famous Bugatti's of the past, including the Type 57 Atlantic coupe, in developing the handsome lines of the EB112 sedan.

In addition to designing everything from cameras to washing machines and running shoes, Giugiaro has designed more than 100 production vehicles and dozens and dozens of concept cars, many of them establishing new benchmarks in surface treatment, vehicle architecture and breakthrough design themes.

Italdesign's first concept was the Bizzarrini Manta, presented at the Turin show in 1968 as a prototype sports car that had three seats, with the driver positioned between the passengers. "The show car or prototype is a way to find and to try out new ideas," says Giugiaro, who was voted the most influential automotive designer of the 20th century. "In a nutshell, it's research, creative thinking and vision." Such vehicles are expensive to design and to build, but, he says, "You do it for pleasure and for joy, hoping to encounter approval and success." And, he adds: "The creative person takes the risk."

142-143 Giugiaro's son, Fabrizio, studied architecture and business, and didn't join Italdesign as a full-time basis until 1994. However, the 1991 Nazca M12 was his first complete concept car project for the company. The BMW-powered Nazca M12 concept made its debut at the Geneva show in 1991, when Fabrizio was 26 years old.

143 top Power for the Nazca M12 came from a BMW V12 engine.

Italdesign had done earlier work for the German marque, designing and producing the famed BMW M1 in 1978. In 1996, Fabrizio Giugiaro was promoted to head of the Styling and Prototype Division of Italdesign.

144 top, center and 145 top The Formula Hammer was a versatile and fun concept presented in 1996 at Turin, where it reminded many of the beloved Fiat Jolly. The Hammer concept could be configured with a variety of body panels, top and side curtains. The Hammer and the Formula 4 both were built around Fiat powertrains.

144 bottom and 145 bottom The Formula 4, which made its debut in Geneva in 1996, has all of its mechanical components housed in its floor pan. The upper body shell is made of strong but lightweight carbon fiber. The concept was designed so the upper shell can be replaced with a roadster or even a van body style. The Formula 4 concept had no doors; the driver and passengers stepped into their cockpits.

146-147 The Alfa Romeo Scighera concept featured aluminum and carbon fiber construction and a 400-horsepower bi-turbocharged V6 engine that could sprint it to 100 km/h in only 3.8 seconds. Giugiaro designed the Scighera for the Geneva show in 1997. While the car looked racy, and had a racecar's dynamic capabilities, its two-seat interior was luxuriously tailored in Connolly leather upholstery.

148 left and 148-149
The Giugiaros knew they were taking a risk when they presented the Alfa Romeo Brera at Geneva in 2002. "My father and I worried before the show that no one would understand it," Fabrizio Giugiaro said of the 400-horsepower sports car. The Giugiaros had nothing to fear. People around the world loved the beautiful concept car. Automotive News, the international newspaper that covers the auto industry, liked the Brera so much it honored its exterior design and selected it as concept car of the year.

148 bottom Giugiaro decided it was time to apply beautiful design to the sport utility vehicle and presented the Maserati Kubang GT Wagon concept at Detroit in 2003. The wagon is named for a Javan wind.

149 bottom and right Kubang's design provides for versatility. The interior can be configured with seating for four or five. The cargo area can hold two more seats or can be extended with the tailgate supporting long items.

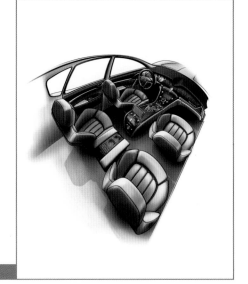

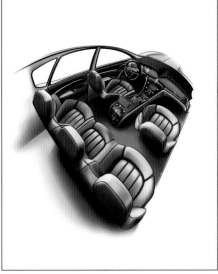

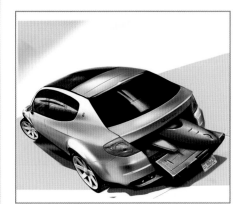

150-151 *Giugiaro's contribution to the 50th anniversary of the Chevrolet Corvette was the Moray concept it presented at the 2003 Geneva show. The car's name revives memories of such Corvette-based concepts as the Mako Shark and Manta Ray, but the Moray adds an Italian interpretation to the lines of the classic American sports car.*

CORVETTE

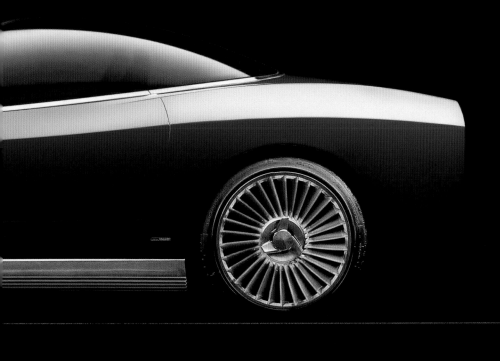

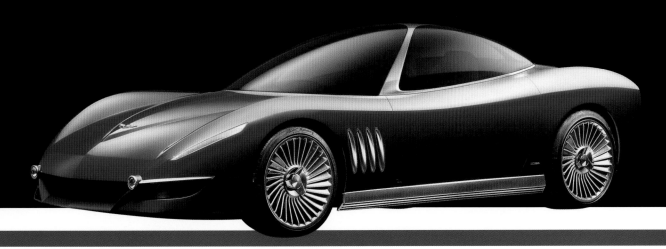

LEONARDO

eonardo Fioravanti raises his right hand to just above eye level, and he holds it there momentarily, long enough that you notice his wrist extending just beyond the impeccably crisp seams of a precisely tailored suit jacket and you realize that the way he positions his hand reminds you of a model posing for Michelangelo himself. But you know that Leonardo Fioravanti is not being pretentious, he's simply sincere in his gesture.

"With this hand," he says, and he says it reverently, "I have the chance to design eight Ferraris."

Around the world, schoolboys draw cars, daydreaming about how much fun, how exciting it would be if those lines suddenly took shape in metal

*152 top and 153 center
The portfolio of Leonardo
Fioravanti includes eight
Ferraris he designed while
working at Pininfarina. The
250 P5 concept car was
shown at Geneva in 1968.*

*152-153 bottom
Fioravanti's production
Ferraris include the V8-
powered 308 GTB
introduced as a 1975
model and the 308 GTS,
which was launched in
1977.*

FIORAVANTI

The essence of Italian style

so they could turn the key and hear the roar of the powerful engine and drive away in their car. "Boys want to be car designers or rock stars," says one American who grew up to live one half of that dream. But even those who live the dream rarely if ever design a Ferrari, yet that's what Leonardo Fioravanti did, and he did it eight times.

Fioravanti's curriculum vitae lists those fabled Ferraris as the Dino 206 GT, the P5, the 365 GTB 4 Daytona, the P6, the 365 GT4 BB Berlinetta Boxer, the 365 GT4 2+2, the 308 GTB and GTS and the 288 GTO, a collection that would be the envy of any car collector, let alone a car designer. But those were just the Ferraris that Fioravanti styled with his right hand. As designer, then project manager, then assistant director,

153 top Leonardo Fioravanti joined Ferrari before launching his own architecture and design studio, which is housed in a 13th Century building on a quaint, cobbled square in the hillside town of Moncalieri, just across the Po River from Turin. Ferraris remain his favorites, but his personal car collection includes a 1952 Citroën, a 1953 Mercedes-Benz, a 1958 Jaguar and a 1966 Lancia that he drives on a regular basis.

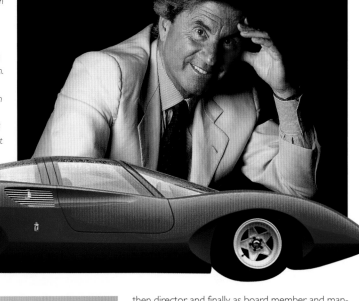

then director and finally as board member and managing director of Pininfarina Studi e Richerche SpA, Fioravanti directed the design of several other Ferraris, as well as assorted Lancias, Alfas, Peugeots, and even a Honda and the Cadillac Allante.

Fioravanti joined Pininfarina soon after securing his degree in mechanical engineering in 1964 from the Milan Polytechnic University, where he specialized in motor vehicle construction and aerodynamics. He worked at Pininfarina for 24 years, until Enzo Ferrari, "il Commendatore Ferrari himself," as Fioravanti puts it, hired him away to become assistant general manager of Ferrari SpA and then the managing director of Ferrari Engineering.

At about that same time, Fioravanti opened his own design consulting business, Fioravanti Srl, to do architectural work on homes and golf course clubhouses in Japan.

After Ferrari's death in the summer of 1988, Fioravanti's role expanded as he became manager of advanced design for Fiat, which several years earlier had added Ferrari to its corporate portfolio. Within a year he was responsible for all design at Fiat Auto. But a year later, he left Fiat to focus on his own business, which he expanded into transportation and industrial design, working exclusively on advanced automotive designs for Fiat and its brands until 1995. Since then, Fioravanti Srl has grown to 60 people, full or part-time, including Fioravanti's sons Matteo (an architect) and Luca (an attorney). Fioravanti Srl has done design work for automakers in North America, Japan and Europe, and also has designed boats, harbor systems, even a fishing reel and a unique bicycle that can be configured for either a male or female rider.

While his corporate work remains confidential, Fioravanti has produced a portfolio of his own concept cars. He deserves praise for their design, for their technical innovation and for his own bravery. Concept cars are very expensive to create. Most design studios have become reluctant to make such an investment without a major automaker underwriting those costs.

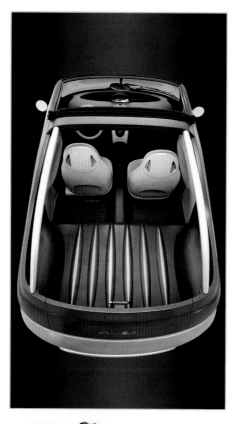

"In my opinion," says Paolo Caccamo, chief executive officer of I.DE.A., one of Italy's "Big Four" design houses, "it does not make sense anymore to do concepts on your own. They are so expensive. We prefer to do them on behalf of the client, or together with the client."

Still, says Giorgetto Giugiaro of Italdesign, doing such concepts on your own allows you "to express our own opinions and ideas in freedom. If there are two partners, you always have to 'compromise,' and the person who has the money is going to be the one who decides. You may please your customer, but you don't please yourself."

While Giugiaro likes working with a corporate partner, his company is large enough that it can afford to do concepts on its own when it wants. "You strive to go in the freest way possible," he explains, adding the warning that when the concept car is totally yours, "you are responsible for the good, and for the bad."

Giugiaro also notes that while a design studio may be paid very well by an automaker for a concept vehicle, when the studio does that concept alone it spends its own money. "In fact, it's very expensive," he

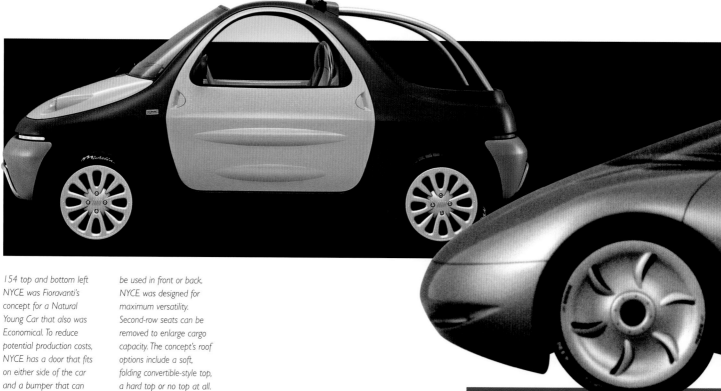

154 top and bottom left NYCE was Fioravanti's concept for a Natural Young Car that also was Economical. To reduce potential production costs, NYCE has a door that fits on either side of the car and a bumper that can be used in front or back. NYCE was designed for maximum versatility. Second-row seats can be removed to enlarge cargo capacity. The concept's roof options include a soft, folding convertible-style top, a hard top or no top at all.

says, "but you do it for pleasure and for joy, hoping to encounter approval and even success. The creative person takes the risk. Maybe a creative person should never run a business. The creative mind comes before everything else. This is very, very Italian."

So is Fioravanti's approach, though with a few exceptions: his personal collection of 15 vehicles and vintage race and rally cars includes a 1953 Mercedes-Benz 220, a 1952 Citroën 11 BL and a 1958 Jaguar 2.4.

"The sense of proportion, good treatment of surface (like Giugiaro, for me, he is the master in the treatment of surface), of things that are beautiful in three dimensions, of fantasy, creativity, of seeing something new in the future, and also the details," Fioravanti says, "that was typically Italian."

Fioravanti presented his first concept in 1994 at the Turin Motor Show, and it was a showcase for both design and technological concepts. Sensiva took its name from tires that use elastomer sensors in their tread to "sense" the road surface, relaying this information to vehicle computer systems that adjust everything from camber to spring rates to power output, providing both speed and safety.

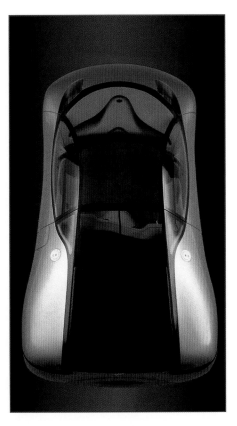

While providing very high performance capabilities, Sensiva also was an environmentally friendly vehicle with a hybrid powertrain. It also introduced a wheel/tire/brake/active suspension unit that heralded Fioravanti's push for standardization of parts.

Fioravanti had two concepts for the next Turin show, in 1996. One — Flair — displayed more practical applications of Sensiva's aerodynamics while the other — NYCE — introduced a new concept in parts standardization. Flair demonstrated how airflow can be used to enhance vehicle dynamics while NYCE, or Natural Young Car and Economical, showcased developments in parts reduction and standardization.

155 top and bottom Fioravanti's first concept car after launching his own studio was Sensiva, unveiled at the Turin show in 1994. Like his concepts that followed, Sensiva was both a design and technological showcase. Sensiva's seats don't move, but the vehicle's pedals adjust to fit the driver. To make sure the driver has optimal peripheral vision, the passenger seat is set slightly back. While tires with road-sensing tread were only a dream when Sensiva was unveiled, technological advances may make such tires feasible in the early years of the 21st century.

In anticipation of the 100th anniversary of Enzo Ferrari's birth, Fioravanti shifted gears with F100, a compact, lightweight but powerful GT concept at the Turin show in 1998. Two years later at Turin he presented the F100r, a roadster version of the car, alongside TRIS, an advanced design based on the NYCE concept.

156-157 F100 was Fioravanti's proposal for the centennial anniversary of the birth of Enzo Ferrari. The concept was presented at the Turin show in 1998. Two years later, Fioravanti built the F100r, a roadster variation designed to minimize turbulence around the driver and passenger. The F100 was designed to carry a V10, Formula One-style engine, wrapped inside a package that shows classic Ferrari styling cues. Inside, the seats include leg supports with built-in pedals for the driver and a footrest for the passenger. Even the F100's wheels are a special concept designed and built in conjunction with Fergat. The goal was a wheel that is beautiful, light yet strong enough to handle the loads required by car's extremely high-speed capability.

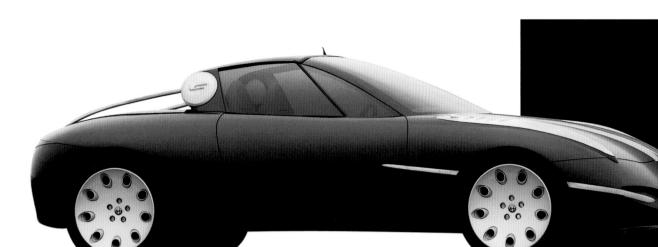

With the demise of Turin's show, Fioravanti and many other Italian design houses moved their premieres to the neutral ground of the annual auto show at Geneva, Switzerland.

Fioravanti's concept for Geneva in 2001 was Vola, a sports coupe that turned into a roadster in a unique way. Rather than folding like origami that is swallowed by the vehicle's trunk, Vola's lightweight roof simply rotated from above the seats to over the trunk.

158-159 Vola is Fioravanti's concept for a roadster with a disappearing hard top. But the roof isn't the only innovation this concept explores. Inside, the driver and passenger sit in specially formed compartments. Vola shows Fioravanti's belief in elegant simplicity. Instead of a complicated mechanism that folds the top and inserts it in the trunk, Vola's roof simply pivots into position above the trunk lid.

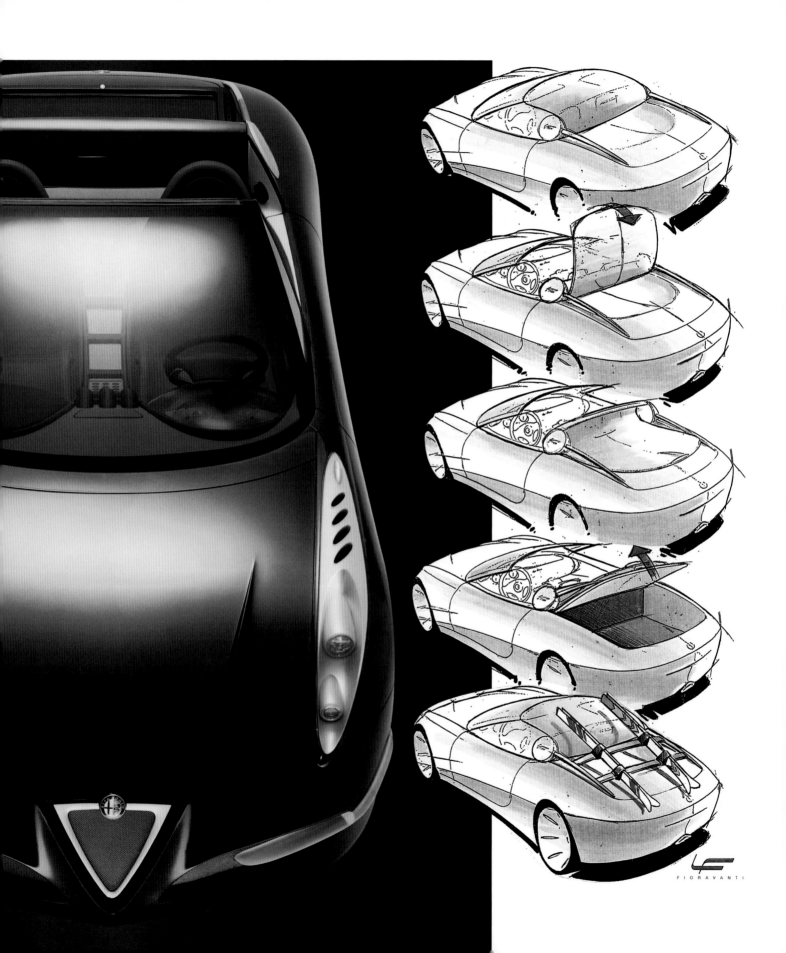

FIORAVANTI

"But why put the roof in the boot?" Fioravanti asks, explaining that the systems currently in use are mechanically complex and heavy, steal from the already very limited cargo space available in the trunks of such cars and affect the vehicle's weight distribution and thus its driving dynamics.

"If you drive quietly, it's not a problem," he explains. "But if you drive fast, it's like driving a different car. The coupe is one car. The cabriolet is another car."

Fioravanti's concept for the Geneva show in 2002 was Yak, a V8-powered, four-wheel-drive, crossover sport utility vehicle that represents a reaction against the fragmentation of the automotive marketplace. "Certain people have asked, 'please give me one car for all my needs,'" Fioravanti explains.

160 top and 161 top Yak is a luxurious sport utility vehicle concept with such innovative features as windshield wipers for the side windows, light-emitting diode headlamps and front-seat armrests that present the driver and passenger with their four-point safety harnesses.

160 center and 160-161 bottom Tris advances on the themes of the NYCE concept. Tris has three interchangeable doors, improving utility while holding down potential production costs. Tris was designed as a concept that could be produced in emerging markets such as Asia or Africa.

"What they want," he says, "is a vehicle with the elevated vantage and go-anywhere capability of an SUV, but with an even more versatile cargo area and the comfort of a luxury sedan."

Yak showcased a variety of innovative features that today may be achieved only through the designer's dream and the creative engineering of a company such as CECOMP (Centro Esperienze Costruzione Modelli e Prototipi), a Turin specialist in the construction of prototype vehicles.

"However," says Fioravanti, "fantasy, creativity and engineering, these are not things in contrast."

For example, he says, when he designed Sensiva it was a designer's concept, with no immediate practical-

ity for production. However, with recent advances in technology, one of the world's major tire makers is working on just such a tire system. Major automakers also have come forward to work with Fioravanti Srl on further development of the NYCE and Yak concepts.

"It is extremely satisfying when you image something and realize this meets the need of another person," Fioravanti says.

"To project," he adds, "is from the Latin, *projectus*. This means to put something forward.

"When you meet the challenge to imagine where things will go, this is the best. Designing for the future means to have a love of new things, to dream, to have fantasy."

CONTEMPORARY

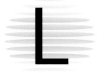

Late in 2002, General Motors brought Harley Earl back from the grave. At least the automaker's advertising agency employed a tall (Earl stood 6 feet 4 inches), fat-tie'd, double-breasted suit-wearing, fedora-topped, two-tone-shoe'd actor who portrayed the man who brought Hollywood hype to Detroit's design for a series of television commercials for GM's Buick brand.

Harley Earl invented the concept car, the styling studio with its clay models and the Motorama, that Broadway show of singing, dancing and heavily chromed design where his dream cars — and GM's newest offerings that you could buy at your local dealership — were displayed to optimistic expectations and to rave reviews.

But what would Harley Earl think about contemporary concept cars and the major international auto shows where they are revealed? Would he be disappointed or delighted? Pleased or perplexed?

Earl, who died in 1969, might be perplexed to see that cars no longer have wings and fins or even very much in the way of chrome, that they still are powered (for the most part) by piston-driven, internal combustion engines and that they haven't become true living rooms on wheels, steering themselves along fully automated highways. He might even wonder why all convertibles don't have tops that close by themselves when it rains, like the 1951 LeSabre concept car that he drove from work to his home and to his country club.

But he'd be pleased, very pleased, by the variety of innovative designs and by the new technologies those designs showcase. However, he likely would be astounded that in addition to designers' dream versions of sedans, coupes, convertibles, sports cars

CONCEPT CARS

What would
Harley Earl
think?

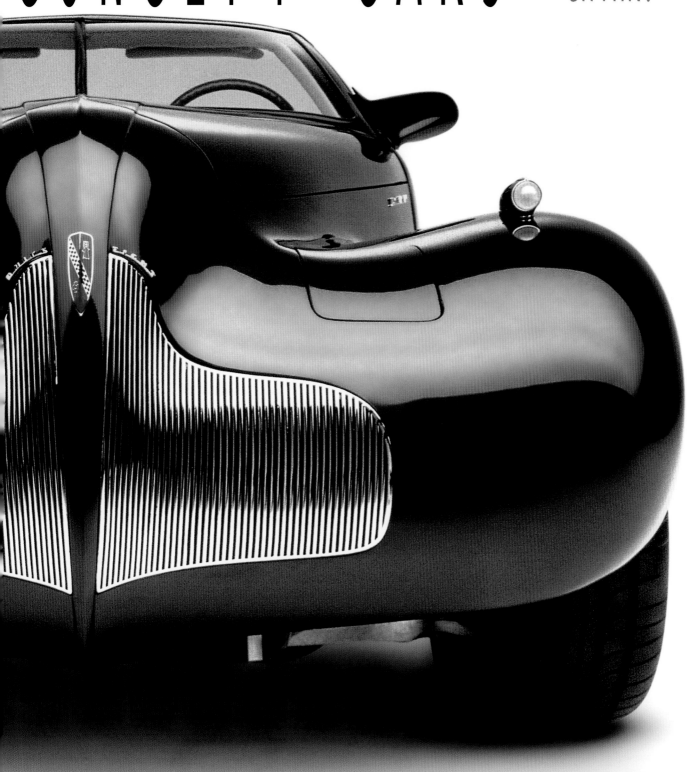

162-163 Would Harley Earl like the Buick Blackhawk? This concept, created in 2000, carries forward styling cues from Earl's Buicks of the 1930s and 1940s. The car even carries a vintage powerplant, a 7.5-liter (455 cubic inch) 1970s Buick V8 tuned to produce more than 460 horsepower.

164-165 Earl's 1938 Buick Y-Job concept had the first power convertible top. The Buick Blackhawk carries a retractable hardtop. Buick commissioned former GM designer Steve Pasteiner to help with the Blackhawk, which uses interior components from a 1996 Buick Riviera.

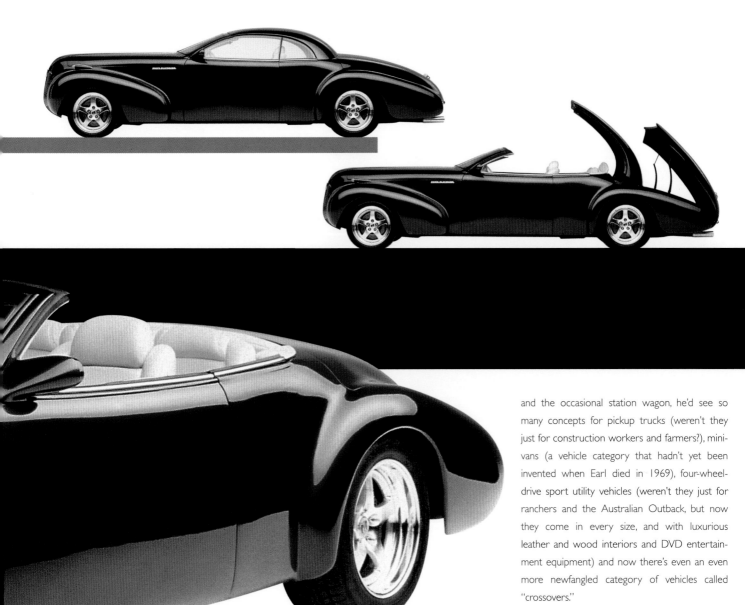

and the occasional station wagon, he'd see so many concepts for pickup trucks (weren't they just for construction workers and farmers?), minivans (a vehicle category that hadn't yet been invented when Earl died in 1969), four-wheel-drive sport utility vehicles (weren't they just for ranchers and the Australian Outback, but now they come in every size, and with luxurious leather and wood interiors and DVD entertainment equipment) and now there's even an even more newfangled category of vehicles called "crossovers."

Earl likely would be distressed by his own company's declining market share. But he'd have to be delighted that automakers around the world have embraced his concept of dream cars and have followed his lead in revealing them with extravagant productions of sight and sound, of surprise and delight.

166-167 The LaCrosse was Buick's official concept car for the auto show circuit in the year 2000. The concept carries such traditional styling cues as portholes on the front quarterpanel and cross-car rear lighting. The LaCrosse looks like an elegant sedan, but its rear lights are part of a tailgate and its rear deck lid slides up beneath the roof panel to create an open cargo bed more than a meter in width. The hood over the LaCrosse's transversely mounted 4.2-liter V8 engine opens to the side with a special hinge mechanism that attaches to the right side of the chassis just ahead of the firewall.

LaCrosse

168 top The Pontiac Division of General Motors showed its G6 concept on the auto show circuit in 2003. The maroon and blue leather interior was designed to provide the look and feel of a sophisticated GT sports sedan, with details such as gauges, dials and switches inspired by active sports gear.

168 bottom For many years, the SS (Super Sport) badge was worn by powerful Chevrolet models. For the 2003 auto show circuit, Chevrolet revived the badge on this concept coupe designed as a modern American muscle car. For the SS, the muscle comes from a 6.0-liter, 430-horsepower V8 engine.

169 top The Pontiac G6 is a concept for an aggressive four-passenger sedan. A supercharged V6 engine provides power to a four-wheel-drive system, but GM's Displacement on Demand technology would enable the car to save fuel by running only three cylinders at cruising speeds.

169 bottom The Chevrolet SS concept rides on 22-inch rear wheels, which house 14.75-inch brake rotors. Many visitors to the Detroit show said the car looked like an American interpretation of a Ferrari, though this would be a large Ferrari with seating inside for five people.

170-171 As its name indicates, the Lamborghini Zagato Raptor was designed by Zagato. The Raptor made its debut at Geneva in 1996. The concept had three interchangeable tops and could be presented as a double-bubble coupe, a roadster with a pair of roll bars or an open single-seater with a hard tonneau over the passenger's seat.

While other manufacturers may not have been quite as prolific as Chrysler, they all now use concept cars to inspire, to entice, to preview and to tell their stories.

"Companies have learned over the years that they can say a lot, can communicate a lot about their business and its direction through concept cars," says Wayne Cherry, who in 1992 became only the fourth person to inherit Harley Earl's mantle as leader of GM Design.

"To me, the best concepts are the ones where you decide what it is that you want to communicate and then you design the concept vehicle to communicate that, because these are a huge communication tools. Throughout history, concept cars have been about communicating.

"The company, the design organization, the engineering organization, there's something they want to say and they can say it pretty clearly, pretty focused, and pretty loudly through concepts.

172-173 top The Venturi Fetish made its debut at Geneva in 2002. The concept was designed by Yugoslavian-born Sacha Lakic, whose family moved to Paris when he was an infant. Lakic made his name as a motorcycle designer but was hired by Venturi Automobiles president Gildo Pallanca Pastor to design the Fetish auto concept.

172-173 bottom Chrysler's Crossfire may be the first on-the-road dividend of the joining of the American company with Mercedes-Benz. The Crossfire concept was designed at Chrysler's Pacifica Studio in southern California, but the production version is built in Germany, by Karmann, using many Mercedes-Benz mechanical components.

"The Y-Job was built on a Buick platform and powertrain, but after the war they built something [the LeSabre] from the ground up. They were sending a message with that vehicle. It was communicating something about General Motors.

"I think we've seen that coming back in the last few years. Companies have something they want to say. They want to show the direction that they're heading in. A concept is a pretty cost-effective way of showing the capabilities of the company, the capability of the design and engineering organizations, and of sending the messages.

"If you look back, there was a period when a lot of people would do show cars primarily just to create a sense of enthusiasm within their design studios. A lot of them were done without a great deal of thought about reality. They were just pieces of styling, with no real intent from the company to build them," says Gerry McGovern, who designed

for Chrysler, Peugeot and Rover before leading the redesign of Ford's Lincoln and Mercury brands.

"But what's happened over the last six, seven or eight years is that people have gotten a lot more realistic about their show cars. You've seen a lot of show cars that have materialized quickly into real vehicles; J's Beetle [the Volkswagen New Beetle co-designed by Ford design boss J Mays] was one that got that ball rolling.

"You do a concept to measure public reaction, and if it's favorable, you want it designed so it doesn't take five or six years to get it into production, so if reaction is good we can almost press the button and have it out there in two or two and a half years."

For years, many concept cars were little more than fiberglass bodies on wooden frames and they were pushed into position for showing. Increasingly, they are real vehicles, designed on computers around real engineering parameters, with functioning

powertrains and suspension, and with possible production in mind. "We look back at the '50s and that stuff generated a great amount of publicity and generated a lot of interest, but how much it actually influenced the real cars is questionable," McGovern notes. "Some of it certainly did, but show cars now, generally, are a lot more serious."

So serious, it seems, that companies are using them not just to titillate, but also to educate customers, and the media, about the essence of the brands, especially when the brands are turning in new directions. "I came into this job and was asked to put an organization together what would, from a design perspective, help transform the image of the brands," says McGovern. "Our show cars test the water and the reaction, but more importantly, they are design exercises to prove to ourselves that the philosophy works from one model to another, and can be applied to different sizes and even to different types of vehicles."

C-AIRDREAM

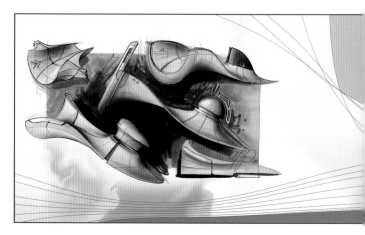

176-177 French automaker Citroën unveiled its C-Airdream concept at the Paris show late in 2002. The concept's design is a showcase of flowing lines and clean contours. By using drive-by-wire technology, Citroën opens space and explores new contours inside this 2+2 coupe concept. Accelerator and braking controls are contained in the steering wheel. Citroën's Hydractive 3 suspension system provides a riding-on-air feeling, but can be switched from comfort to a sport mode when the driver wants to explore the potential of 200-horsepower V6 engine.

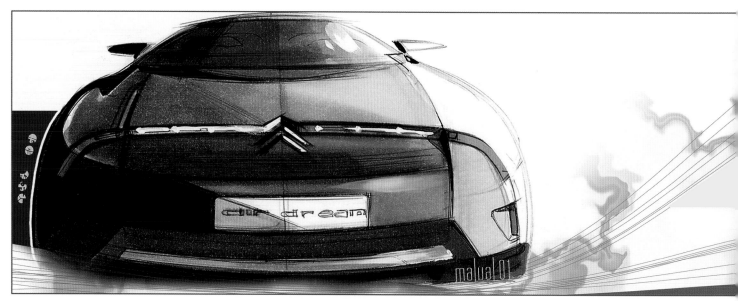

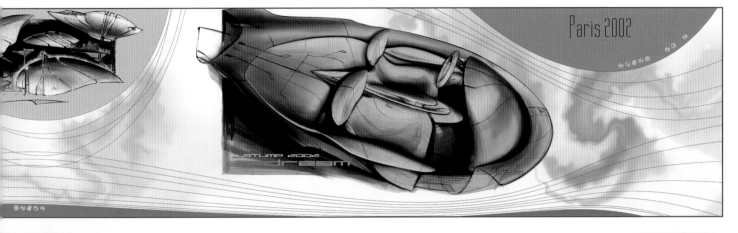

178-179 The Citroën
C-Airdream's roof tapers
until its abrupt conclusion
between broad rear
shoulders. The concept's
grille is designed around
Citroën's dual chevron logo.

The C-Airdream's all-glass
roof provides a panoramic
view for those riding inside
the 2+2 coupe concept.
The play of light was one
of the themes for the car's
interior design.

Thus after doing the Lincoln Mark IX and Continental, both large cars, McGovern's newest concept was for a smaller Lincoln Navicross, yet one that shows the same design directions, and he and his staff have started a similar effort to show the new styling themes for Mercury.

Wayne Cherry notes that General Motors followed a similar strategy when it redesigned its Cadillac brand with an "art and science" styling theme. In 1999, Cadillac unveiled Evoq, a concept for a roadster. A year later, it rolled out Imaj, a limousine or large sedan concept. In 2001, it presented Vision, a wagon concept. In 2002, it added Cien, a V12-powered supercar concept.

"We took four very different kinds of vehicles and showed how the new Cadillac design philosophy would look, where we wanted Cadillac to go in the future," Cherry explains. "You might see something in a single concept, but when you see three or four of them, you really get it, you really understand that this is the direction."

Renault has made a similar, carefully crafted strategic presentation of its new design theme, which has been introduced through the Vel Satis, Avantime, Talisman and Ellypse concepts and the Megane II production cars.

Hyundai's HCD (Hyundai California Design) series of concepts has shown a similar progression on a corporate styling theme, first on a sports coupe concept, then with a luxury sedan and a pair of crossover vehicles.

But not everyone charts such a long-term course to educate the car-buying public. In 1989, radical freelance product designer Luigi Coloni wanted to shock the world's automakers and their designers and went

on a worldwide barnstorming tour — Automorrow — with more than a dozen concept vehicles, all part of his "Utah" series that ranged from a needle-like motorcycle through a series of bat-like cars to a bug-eyed transport truck. The late '80s were a time of many such radical designs from independent studios that pushed the edges of the automotive envelope. Like Coloni, Franco Sbarro's Swiss styling studio and IAD (International Automotive Design) of Britain were exploring extreme shapes and Giugiaro's Italdesign was examining amazing new surface details.

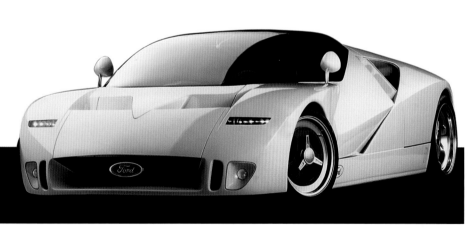

While many concept cars were well-disguised precursors to upcoming production vehicles, the excitement focused on the concept car themes that went toward the extremes.

At one end were exotic, road-going racecars, cars that looked like they could be driven from the driveway in front of your house to the starting grid at Le Mans. These concepts included the Mercedes-Benz C112, Italdesign's Nazca M12, the Ford GT90 and many more.

Also operating that the high-powered end of the concept car spectrum were large, ultra-luxury vehicles — huge and awesomely equipped sedans and GT cars such as the Maybach and Morgan Aero 8.

The Maybach and Morgan also represented another trend — cars that rekindled memories for famous marques, whether it was a New Beetle for Volkswagen or a new Thunderbird for Ford, or the rebirth of a brand, such as Bugatti or Morgan.

182 top Mercedes-Benz showed the concept car for its new ultra-luxury Maybach line at Tokyo in 1997. The V12-powered production version was unveiled at the Paris show in 2002. The car has two models, the 62 (which is 6.17 meters in length) and the 57 (a mere 5.73 meters from bumper to bumper).

182 bottom In 1995, Ford applied its "new edge" design theme as it paid homage to its Le Mans-winning GT40 racecar with the Ford GT90 concept. Beneath the GT90's angular shell are mechanical components from the Jaguar XJ200 supercar.

182-183 Mercedes-Benz rekindled memories of its C111 concept series when it presented the gull-winged C112 experimental car at the Frankfurt show in 1991. The C112 drew inspiration and some of its components from the Sauber-Mercedes C11 racecars.

At the other end of this dream car exercise were small and fuel efficient yet very interesting cars, especially those that placed exotic bodies on a company's entry-level chassis, vehicles such as the Peugeot Asphalte, built on the 106 platform, or a whole series of concepts that Fiat commissioned off its Bravo/Brava chassis. Patrick Le Quement, who left Ford to become s head of design at Renault in 1987, used the French company's Matra subsidiary to build particularly interesting concepts, including a couple of small city cars with pivoting rear axles so they shrink themselves for tighter parking.

184-185 Renault took styling cues it introduced on VelSatis, its first internally created concept car under Patrick Le Quement's reign, and applied them to minivan architecture to create Avantime, which made its debut at Geneva in 1999.

185 top A Renault designer works on sketches for the Initiale concept in 1995. The sedan was developed with a hatchback design that built on the tradition of the Renault 16 and Safrane. Because of its luxurious nature, it included specially created luggage from Louis Vuitton, seats covered in Scottish leather and a champagne holder.

184 top Renault's concept car for the Frankfurt show in 1995 was a large, powerful sedan called the Initiale, which was known within the company's design studio by its code name, the Z06, when it was going through the design and modeling phases of its development.

184 bottom A designer works with a wire frame outline to examine component-packaging options inside the shape of the Initiale concept, which carried a detuned version of Renault's 3.5-liter Formula One racing engine.

185 bottom Patrick Le
Quement left Ford's design
studio in 1987 to lead the
transition of the Renault studio
from one that did styling —
basically forming shapes around
mechanical components — to
one that does true vehicle
design. Le Quement's power
within Renault is considered
the strongest of any
automaker's design director

Other European automakers (as well as watch-maker Swatch) and the Japanese manufacturers also were seeking exposure for their innovative ideas for micro cars.

Toyota, Nissan and Mazda had shown concept vehicles as early as 1970, but the Japanese really got into the dream car game in the late 1980s and early '90s. With styling studios in Europe and California and with ties to General Motors and Lotus, Isuzu presented a series of design studies, including a stylish pickup truck with a Formula One racing engine and a car that also was a boat; the idea being that those stuck in Tokyo traffic could navigate the city's waterways instead of its clogged highways.

186 top, 186-187 and 187 top left Matra designers drew their inspiration for the Matra P57 concept car from the famous Bugatti Type 35 racing cars of the late 1920s. The Matra prototype is part car, part motorcycle. Like a motorcycle, the car is narrow and its four wheels are not enclosed within the bodywork.

187 top right Mercedes-Benz and watchmaker Swatch were partners in the early days of the development of the MCC (Micro Compact Car) Smart car concept, which became a wholly owned DaimlerChrysler enterprise in 1998.

188 top Matra produced sports cars and its racing teams won Formula One and Le Mans championships. Since the mid 1970s, the company has concentrated on the design and manufacture of vehicles for the street. Matra designers have created some 100 concept cars and led the development of the European minivan.

188-189 and 189 top left Matra created its P75 concept for the Michelin Challenge Design program for the 2003 Detroit auto show.

189 top right and bottom right P75 is designed as an urban vehicle with an environmentally friendly electric powertrain. It has compact exterior dimensions but a roomy interior for four people or for the transportation and delivery of cargo. The P75 has a light but rigid stainless steel chassis that carries all mechanical components below its low floor. The concept's body is made from sheet-molded compound. The rear doors have a special hinge system to ease access in tight spaces.

Mitsubishi's HSR (Human Science Research) concepts provided exotic bodies on chassis that were test beds for advanced technology. Honda concepts were rare, and often were designed to showcase hybrid powertrains that combined an electric motor with a small internal combustion engine to provide transport with less pollution.

Even such "green" vehicles had their concept car extremes. Honda's Dualnote was an interesting concept: a sports car with a 400-horsepower hybrid powertrain. I.DE.A. worked with a Japanese university to develop a high-speed, eight-wheeled electric vehicle. General Motors recruited aviation pioneer Burt Rutan to help develop its 100 miles per gallon 1992 Ultralite concept. Ford displayed its radically styled, 80-mpg Synergy 2010 in 1996.

But miles per gallon may become a distant concept if the automakers are correct in their belief that fuel cells will provide the power for the future. Basically, fuel cells are a special form of battery that uses hydrogen and oxygen to produce electrical energy. Instead of the various pollutants that emerge from the tail pipe of a car with an internal combustion engine, fuel cell vehicles leave only water and heat in their wake.

Several car companies have shown fuel-cell concepts. Some even have small fleets of fuel cell-pow-

ered vehicles on the road. But General Motors has used the fuel cell as a springboard to a concept vehicle that's even more radical than Harley Earl's Y-Job.

"One of the things that we had thought about, that I had our advanced group working on, sort of on a back-burner basis, was what if we were to do a Firebird today?" says Wayne Cherry. "There's a whole different set of values. There's a whole different set of influences. It's a whole different world. What would that vehicle look like?

"Of course," Cherry continues, while his designers were thinking about a new Firebird for the 21st century, "the General Motors research and development group has been working on fuel cells and they were thinking about what would be a way to communicate that work. Up until that point, fuel cells were always put into conventional vehicles, and the only way you knew they were fuel cell vehicles, other than the fact that they didn't make any noise, was the fact that they wrote on the side of the car that they were powered by fuel cell."

If the fuel cell was going to provide a new means of transportation, why not make this new Firebird a new mode of transportation?

"Designers always feel they work under restraints," Cherry says. "I told the design team, 'hey, you don't have any restrictions now. Have at it!'"

41,3 in

41,3 in

47,2 in

19,7 in

69 in

21,6 in

140 in

vincent OLIVIER MATRA AUTOMOBILE

MATRA

P75

Former Nissan design manager Jerry Hirshberg says that concept cars "should be three-dimensional questions that ask what if?" That's precisely the question General Motors wanted to answer with its new Firebird, its AUTOnomy concept car. "We started with the premise, 'What if we were inventing the automobile today rather than a century ago?'" said GM president Rick Wagoner as he unveiled AUTOnomy at the North American International Auto Show in Detroit in 2002. "AUTOnomy is more than just a new concept car; it's potentially the start of a revolution in how automobiles are designed, built and used." AUTOnomy includes a chassis that looks like a large skateboard and which houses the fuel-cell propulsion system and the electric motors that drive each of the four wheels, as well as all of the drive-by-wire systems that control steering, braking, power transmission and even climate and entertainment equipment. The skateboard also provides attachment points for the vehicle's bodies.

190 To celebrate its success in the Paris-Dakar rally, Mitsubishi created the Montero Evolution concept vehicle for the 2002 auto show circuit. The concept also extended the company's success. The racing version based on the Evo swept the top four places in the endurance test in 2003. The Montero Evolution's interior (above) was carefully conceived to provide features needed both in town and out on the desert sands. Beneath its hatchback was a drawer equipped for any emergency, with a first-aid kit and a complete set of tools.

191 While most sport utility vehicles have four doors and styling reminiscent of a brick, the Montero Evolution put Mitsubishi's advanced off-road technologies and its high-output 3.5-liter V6 engine on 22-inch wheels, then wrapped them inside the athletic body of a fastback coupe. The Montero concept was among the first projects completed under Mitsubishi design director Olivier Boulay, and was a stunning contrast to the Maybach luxury sedan that he had designed while heading the Mercedes-Benz advanced design studio in Japan from 1992-98.

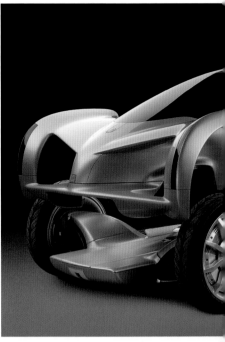

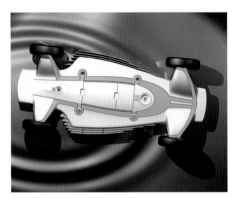

Because of its revolutionary architecture, the AUTOnomy skateboard can carry any type of vehicle body, from a two-seat open roadster to a sedan or minivan to a sport utility or a pickup truck.

After its debut at Detroit wearing a body designed as a two-seat sports car for the year 2020, the AUTOnomy reappeared in the fall at the Paris show as the Hy-Wire, now with its fuel-cell skateboard carrying the body of a five-passenger luxury sedan. That body was built in Turin by Bertone and showcased the latest drive-by-wire technologies from by Sweden's SKF Group.

Just as Harley Earl's Y-Job set standards and goals for designers and engineers for years to come, the AUTOnomy may be the precursor to the future of automotive transportation.

Or, like those original Firebirds, this concept may be nothing more than an optimistic dream, though a dream that makes people think, that pushes everyone toward progress. "Designers love to do concepts. They just love to do concepts," says Wayne Cherry. "It shows the capability. It happens quickly. You got it out in public and get reaction. It's like the opening night of a Broadway or

West End London play, where the media gets a chance to talk and to react, and the other designers get a chance to react, too. It's good impact, good directional sensibility, just sort of testing different types of configurations, different types of bodies, different form vocabularies, different ways to communicate your brand character. And even more important, it presents the message from the company that these are some of the things we're thinking about, and it asks, 'what do you think?'" Harley Earl can't tell us what he thinks, but we think he'd like what he sees.

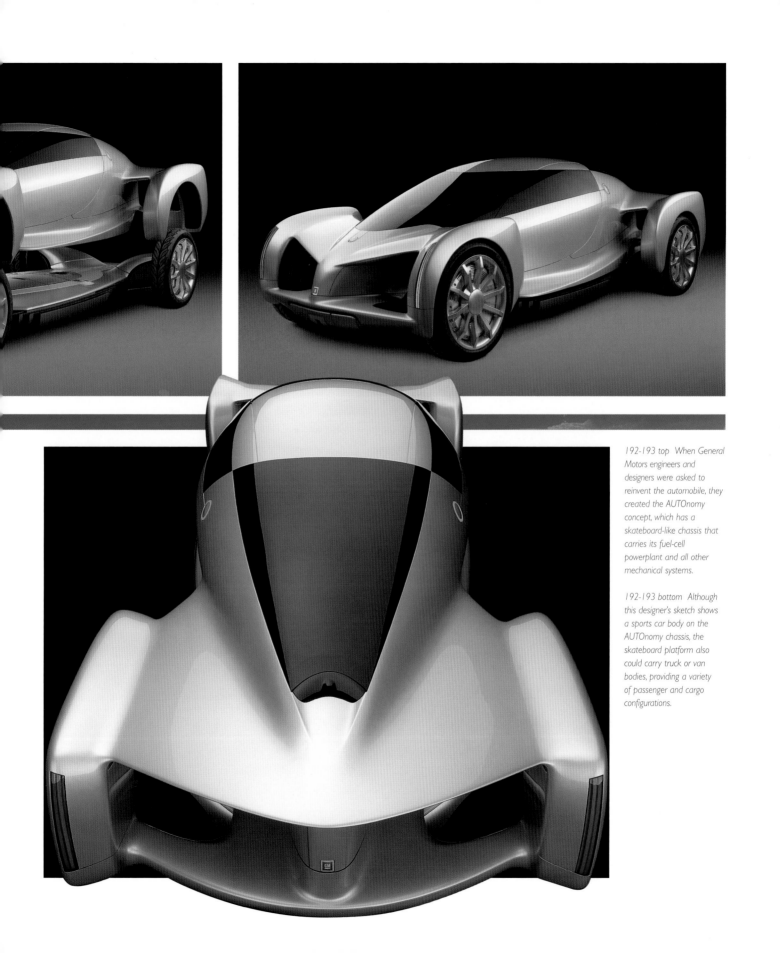

192-193 top When General Motors engineers and designers were asked to reinvent the automobile, they created the AUTOnomy concept, which has a skateboard-like chassis that carries its fuel-cell powerplant and all other mechanical systems.

192-193 bottom Although this designer's sketch shows a sports car body on the AUTOnomy chassis, the skateboard platform also could carry truck or van bodies, providing a variety of passenger and cargo configurations.

J MAYS

Concept cars in a cultural context

JMays has been criticized for gazing too long into the rearview mirror, for pondering the past instead of pushing the future. Yet he's also been accused — and by the many of the same critics — of turning his back on the very past that he supposedly so treasures and of selling off precious family jewels.

Such scorn was directed at Mays in the summer of 2002 when he directed the sale of more than 50 Ford concept cars, most of them the work of the Ghia studio, the famed Italian coach builder and design house founded in 1915. Ford bought Ghia in 1973 but early in 2001 it released 95 percent of the work force. It appeared that Ford was washing its hands of its association with the Italian studio that had created many spectacular concepts but less than a handful of cars that ever made it onto Ford's assembly lines.

"I wasn't here in those years, but Ghia and Filippo Sabino did a lot of great work for Ford," says Mays. "The sale was my idea. The cars were rotting away in a warehouse and the budget wasn't there to keep them the way I wanted to keep them and I knew that we had doubles of about 80 percent of the ones we sold, so I said why don't we sell them and raise some money for charity? We ended up raising $4.3 million for charity, which is great, and it gave everybody a once in a lifetime chance to look at all of these concepts under one roof. It was a very nice event.

"But all the journalists who hadn't thought about these cars in 30 years got a week's worth of heartburn. There was criticism that we were selling the family jewels. It wasn't a case of us not appreciating our past. We were mostly interested in bringing the cars out from under the dust covers and presenting them to the public again."

194 The Indigo draws on Ford's history in competition (thus its name "Indy go" is not just a description of a dark blue color). This "street-legal" concept car was unveiled at the Detroit show in 1996. Ford created two static models and one running prototype. The static models were offered at Ford concept car sale in 2002.

195 The Ghia IXG was designed by Tom Tjaarda, who at the time was an American university student (but also son of Lincoln Zephyr designer John Tjaarda). In 1960 he developed the IXG as an aerodynamic exercise, shaping even the low-slung car's underbody to enhance its stability at high speeds.

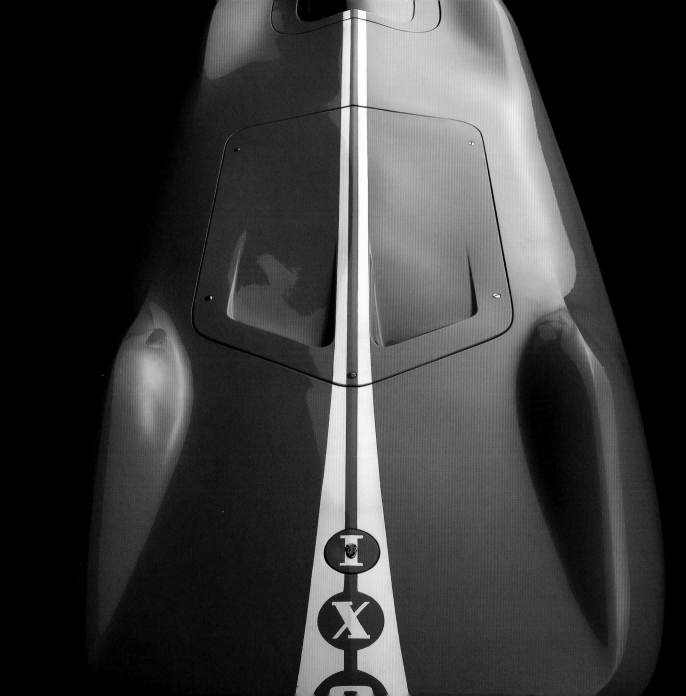

196-197 When the Ghia
Ford Focus concept was
offered at the Ford auction
in 2002, this stunning
example of the automobile
as sculpture drew a bid in

excess of $1.1 million.
The Ghia Focus made its
debut at the Turin show in
1992. Abstract furniture
provided inspiration for
Taru Lahti, a young

designer assigned by Ford
to the Italian studio. Among
the Focus' sculptural details
are its stand-apart
protective side molding
and its dramatic use

of biomechanical shapes.
The concept's interior is
made of steel laminated
with teakwood and has
seats covered with natural
saddle cowhide.

Then there are those who wonder why, as vice president of design for the Ford Motor Company, and thus the person responsible for shaping not only the cars built under Ford's blue oval but also those by Jaguar, Volvo, Aston Martin, Mazda, Mercury, Lincoln and Land Rover, Mays seems to have spent so much of this time designing the cars that people want but can't have (for example, the Ford Forty-Nine) instead of the cars that people can have but don't necessarily want (for example, the Ford Taurus).

Despite such criticism, or perhaps because of it, Mays has become the most well known American car designer since Harley Earl and — ironically — perhaps the most acclaimed ever. In 2002, officials of the Harvard Graduate School selected Mays as only the fourth person to receive their Excellence in Design Award, and the others also were controversial risk-takers: architectural and design superstar Philippe Starck, designer and performing artist Robert Wilson and fashion designer Rei Kawakubo.

The accolades from Harvard inspired an exhibition of Mays' work at the Museum of Contemporary Art in Los Angeles. That exhibit, believed to be the first such extensive presentation of any car designer's work by a major art museum, was called "Retro*futurism*: The Car Design of J Mays."

Retro*futurism*? In an interview for the museum's book on the exhibition, Mays explained that, "the incorporation of 'heritage' into my design approach is a reaction to the confusion and inconsistency created by the fact that for many years cars radically changed in appearance with each new model. My work is an attempt to create visual consistency within a brand as a way to build faith in the brand." Brooke Hodge, curator of architecture and design at the MOCA and organizer of the exhibit, notes that, "Mays' incorpora-

tion of retrofuturism into his creative process has enabled him to draw from the past and design for the future, while remaining firmly grounded in the present.

"Mays' ability to think across the spectrum of design and, in particular, his knowledge of architecture, fashion and industrial design, is what sets him apart from other automotive designers," she adds.

Actually, what seems to set Mays apart from other car designers — other than the amazing breath of his work that ranges from the Audi Avus to the MA concept he designed specifically for the MOCA exhibit — is the way he fits cars into a cultural context.

198-199 The appearance of the Audi Avus at the Tokyo show in 1991 came as an absolute surprise and the design of the spectacular concept made J Mays an international automotive design superstar. The car, which takes its name from a 1930s Berlin racing circuit, had a polished aluminum body with doors that scissored open. The streamlined car introduced the W engine configuration, with 12 cylinders arranged in three banks of four. The 6.0-liter engine produced more than 500 horsepower. Audi claimed a 0-100 kilometers/hour sprint time of only three seconds and a top speed in excess of 200 miles per hour.

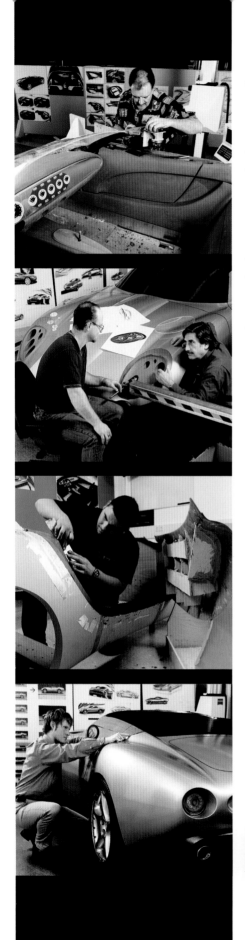

"I don't think the question is 'do I or other designers do vehicles that look backward'," Mays contends, "but 'why do people like those vehicles so much?'

"The dream machines of the '50s were very symptomatic of the mindset of the culture at the time they were created," he explains. "If you look at the concept cars of the late '50s, they were very naive but incredibly exuberant. They looked 40 or 50 years into the future, which is really where the mindset of that culture was at the time.

"They were fascinated with the future. There were those three-wheeled gyroscopic cars and there were levitation vehicles and there was all sorts of stuff and all of that was just the exuberance of the designers trying to portray a world that the public was demanding. The public wanted that stuff. If the public fascination was with a helicopter in every garage, then that's why you saw it written about in *Popular Science* and that's why you saw it at the auto shows.

200 left Many hands were involved in the creation of the Jaguar F-type concept that made its debut at Detroit in 2000. There were the hands of its designers, who included the late Geoff Lawson as well as Jaguar's Keith Helfet, Ian Callum and J Mays, and those of the detail designers and craftsmen working in the Jaguar concept development center to build the prototype.

"The dream machines of the '50s, they were just the dreaming of designers, designers dreaming naïvely sometimes. They disappeared as our fascination with the future disappeared… Now the most into the future we go in today's society is to wonder what's on at the multiplex [movie theater] this weekend? We don't have that same fascination with the future that society did in those days."

In fact, Mays continues in an interview some 14 months after the destruction of the World Trade Center, "It's a pretty screwed up world at the moment and the future looks pretty insecure to all

200-201 and 201 top
Designers had a Jaguar E-type
Lightweight racing car sitting in
their studio to provide

inspiration and an example of
the kind of essential simplicity
they wanted in Jaguar's new
roadster concept. The success

of their efforts shows in the way
the proportions and lines of the
F-type concept reflects so well
against an original E-type (above).

of us. It's unknown. It's not this rosy, gleaming future that was portrayed to us in the '50s.

"There's terrorism. There's chemical warfare. There are all sorts of things we want to shelter our families from. And so the past is a very comfortable place in many respects, and not just in car design. In architecture and fashion and in many aspects of our culture."

Talk with Mays for more than a few minutes and you wonder if he's designing cars or dissecting cultures.

"Ninety percent is having a pulse on culture," he says of his role.

"Designing the aesthetic aspect of the car is easy. There's nothing to that. It's very easy to design a car. What's hard is finding a story to tell. I often make the analogy between the car industry and the movie industry. If you don't have a story, you don't have a movie, and if you don't have a story, you don't have a car, either.

"Cars only become attractive when they become meaningful for people. You have to find a story that has meaning in some way, shape or form for the audience for which you're designing it.

"Harley Earl understood that. He had a sense of theater like very few before or after him."

So should future automotive designers study design or sociology, or perhaps even the cinema?

"They should do all of that," Mays responds. "They should be really good spies. I always tell my guys, the men and women in our design studios, that the designer with the most information is going to win, because that increases your ability to edit a palate that you ultimately want to use."

202-203 The Ford GT40 was the racecar that beat Ferrari at Le Mans in the 1960s, making Ford the first American automaker to win the historic event. In 2002 at the Detroit show, Ford "reissued" the car, in updated form, as a concept vehicle. Ford built several versions of the GT40 concept, including this one that wears the orange and blue colors of the Gulf Oil-sponsored racer. In the weeks after the Detroit show, Ford announced plans to do a limited production run of Ford GT cars based on the GT40 concept.

The curators at Harvard celebrated Mays' ability "to overlay emotional content upon a form vocabulary. This form vocabulary arises from a carefully scripted lexicon as well as from cultural cues derived from brand heritage and contemporary pop culture. The result is a body of work in which form and content are inextricably united in equal measure, provoking an emotional reaction at every point of contact."

Mays' designs have evoked emotional reactions ever since he burst on the international automotive consciousness in 1991 when Audi unveiled its Mays-designed Avus concept at the Tokyo show.

Mays grew up in small-town Oklahoma, where his father farmed and ran an auto parts store. Mays went to the University of Oklahoma, then to Art Center in Pasadena, California. He joined Audi's design staff in 1980, left for BMW in 1983 but returned a year later.

Working with the title of senior designer, Mays was involved in several important programs, including the Avus concept, a concept car so stunning with its polished aluminum body that it appeared not only on the front of many automotive magazines but on the cover of Gregory Janicki's book, *Cars Europe Never Built: Fifty Years of Experimental Cars.*

The Avus drew its inspiration from the streamlined Auto Union racing cars of the 1930s, but represented a breakthrough in lightweight aluminum body construction, and its 12-cylinder engine with its pistons in W-shaped formation instead of the traditional V looked well into the future.

By the time Avus was unveiled, Mays was working in California, as head of Volkswagen's American design center, where he and Freeman Thomas designed Concept 1, which was unveiled to such a popular response at Detroit in 1994 that Volkswagen

had little choice but to put this New Beetle into production.

Mays went back to Germany with Audi in 1993, in charge of Audi's international design strategy, but in 1995 he returned to the United States, helping to direct the New Beetle's launch and doing other branding projects at SHR Perceptual Management of Scottsdale, Arizona.

In 1997, he succeeded Jack Telnack as vice president of design at Ford, and with Ford's expanding group of brands he helped craft concepts ranging from the Jaguar F-type and Volvo's Safety Car to Mercury's MC4 and Lincoln's Mk 9 as well as Ford's Thunderbird, 24.7, Forty-Nine, 427, GT40 and 021C, for which he commissioned furniture designer Mark Newson to do his first automotive study.

Mays' interest in cultures extends across the Ford family of brands and he notes that "understanding

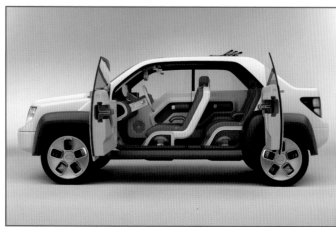

different cultures and different contexts in which cars are designed is part of understanding the design process," which is why Ford opened a new design center in London, because "you can't design a Jaguar in the middle of Dearborn, Michigan. It's impossible."

For the MOCA, Mays designed the MA, which he says is named for the Asian philosophy of "the space between," the threshold where two concepts exist in a mutually beneficial relationship. In the case of the MA car, that space is the area between emotional and rational, between art and science. "It's all about proposing solutions that are not obvious," Mays says, "that are between our traditional visions for a car."

MA is a car you build yourself, a concept designed as a 500-piece kit ready for assembly. The body is made from bamboo, aluminum and carbon fiber, held together by 364 titanium bolts.

204 left Although it looks nothing like the famous Model T, the Ford Model U concept draws on the T's heritage of being a car so versatile it might meet the needs of most drivers. However, the Model U also meets the needs of the environment.

204-205 Model U may have a tough appearance, but some of its body components are made from such things as soy-based resin and corn-based fibers. Corn also provides tire filler. Seats use soy-based foam and the supercharged, hydrogen-fueled internal combustion engine is lubricated by sunflower oil.

205 right The Model U has a reconfigurable interior that can accommodate people or cargo, and even its exterior offers the flexibility of a retractable canvas roof, folding rear window and tailgate that opens to expand cargo capacity. Seats and other internal components lock into slots for easy reconfiguration, and for easy upgrading of technological modules. Many controls are voice-activated. The rear-view mirrors have forward-facing cameras so the driver can see ahead around larger vehicles.

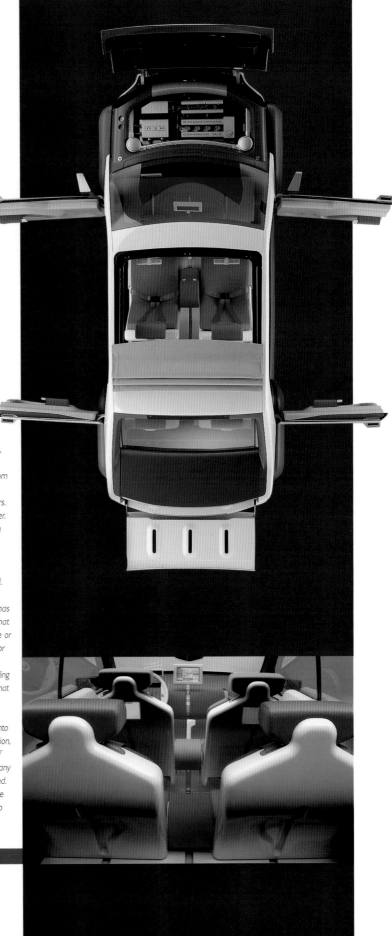

206 J Mays created the MA concept for the Retrofuturism exhibit of his automotive designs as the Museum of Contemporary Art in Los Angeles.

207 MA is designed as a built-it-yourself car kit with its 500 pieces ready for home assembly, and packaged much like the plastic glue-together model cars we built when we were youngsters. Materials used to construct MA include bamboo, aluminum and carbon fiber, held in place with 364 titanium bolts. MA is designed for two people, and can accommodate an electric motor or a small gasoline engine.

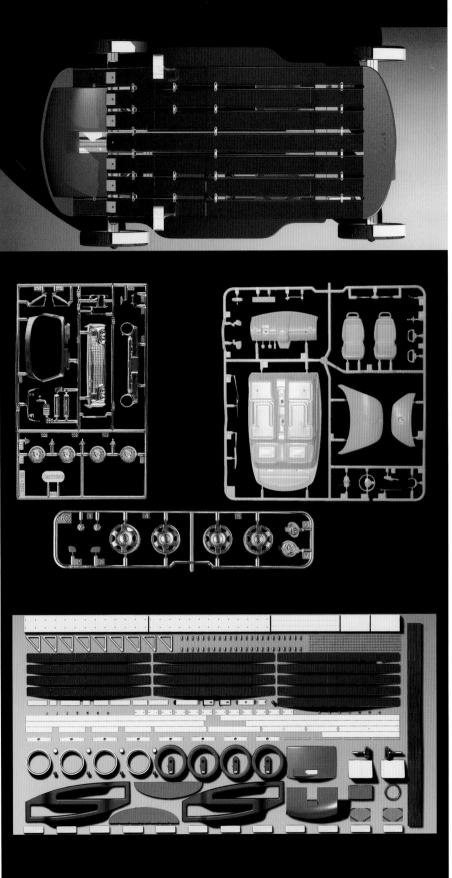

The car is powered by an electric motor and is 96 percent recyclable. MA was designed specifically for the MOCA exhibition.

"We get a lot of 'design for' in the business today," Mays notes. "We get design for functionality and design for manufacturability and we get design for this and design for that and I keep harping to the organization that what we should be thinking about is design for salability, because that's what we do, we sell beautiful cars to our customers, so they have to be desirable.

"I'm not a very fashionable person. I'm actually anti fashion. When I look at something that's going to appeal to a customer, I'm far less interested in transient fashion than I am in enduring longevity and classic values, because I think those are what will continue to live long after the fashionable design's been forgotten.

"I think I have reasonably good taste and I like to think that I understand what the taste of the customer is, and my job is to envision the future on behalf of the customer, and they vote with their dollars, and if they vote no, then you won't be seeing me."

THE ROAD AHEAD

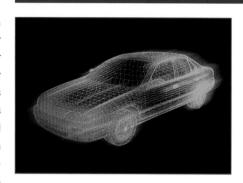

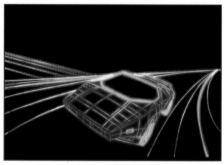

From the very beginning, from the debut of Harley Earl's Y-Job, a vehicle that for its day featured radically sleek styling and introduced such revolutionary features as power windows and a convertible top that retracts at the touch of a button, concept cars have predicted a brighter and better automotive future. These "dream machines" with their new designs and their technological innovations have inspired generations of drivers to ride along eagerly as they await the day when they finally climb behind the wheel — or will it be behind the computerized, joy-stick or twist-and-squeeze "man/machine interface" control unit? — and drive such vehicles themselves. But where are the newest concept cars taking us? What are the problems that designers and engineers are trying to solve with these three-dimensional sculptures that ask the question "what if?" If the millennial AUTOnomy concept is leading us along the road to sustained autonomy and a hydrogen-based economy, what avenue are we to explore in the 1,000-horsepower Cadillac Sixteen concept that AUTOnomy's makers unveiled early in 2003?

"Every period has a vision of the future, but it doesn't always crystallize," cautions Giorgetto Giugiaro, the man honored as the most influential car designer of the 20th Century. "When I joined FIAT in 1965, I was 17 years old and saw a magazine with concept cars created by the Americans," Giugiaro says as he recalls vehicles with turbine engines, even nuclear powerplants, and bizarre bodies with big, aircraft-style wings that supposedly predicted future automotive realities that would turn highways into automated runaways for land-bound craft. "Now, to compare them to cars 40 years later, it was all wrong.

"Everything updates as you move ahead," notes Giugiaro. "Long-term vision is very utopian. Tastes and technology have changed. I am not a medium. I cannot look far into the future. You can't see more than five or 10 years. If you go further than that, it's just a game that you're playing at."

Still, everyone seems eager to play, even Giugiaro, who offers his own ideas about the future of concept car design: "The future is rich for different types of cars," he suggests, comparing modern automotive appetites to those that followed the austere conditions of World War II. "After the second world war, you didn't want just a slice of bread," he says. "You desired a variety of cakes. You wanted to feast your eyes on a whole range of choices."

Likewise, "Carmakers have to please a vast range of tastes. They have to make so many different things. Once a carmaker could make three or four ranges. Now they must do everything. Cars with two seats, with five seats, with seven seats…" Note that Giugiaro speaks in terms of number of seats, not about such things as body style or shape, or even the presence of fenders or the angle of windshields or the ways in which the doors open.

Automakers, says Giugiaro, need a full menu of

vehicles. Tiny cars for crowded urban streets and parking places. But also sedans and coupes. Economy cars and family cars. Luxury cars and ultra-luxury cars. Convertibles and sports cars. Even pickup trucks and especially sport utilities. And luxury sport utilities. And crossovers. Vehicles for every lifestyle. Vehicles for every road surface. Vehicles for every fuel source. And who knows what other architectures and means of propulsion are yet to be developed?

"And tastes change," Giugiaro reminds. "Our way of looking at things changes. Life changes. It's a creative evolution."

For example, he says, recall the period of time when a vehicle's ride height was determined by the quality of the road surfaces. Cars had to be tall enough to provide room for adequate suspension and seat cushioning so driver and passengers could be comfortable. But as roads improved, and as technology improved in everything from suspension to the foam inside those seats, cars could be made lower and sleeker, faster and more maneuverable.

But like those cars, times didn't stand still. Many people began to feel vulnerable and exposed as the volume of traffic increased. People realized that they preferred the sense of protection and strength and the

208 right Changes to a vehicle's design can be made quickly through the computer. Computer programs can be used for analysis by engineers and can even put a vehicle, or at least it's electronic image, into motion.

209 top Virtual-reality technology places designers and ergonomic engineers inside their vehicles, allowing them to see and to feel a car and its equipment long before any hard parts have been fabricated.

209 bottom Computer screens are replacing drawing boards in automotive design studios. Computer-aided design (CAD) technology produces both visual images and computer code that can be used to speed the creation of tangible models.

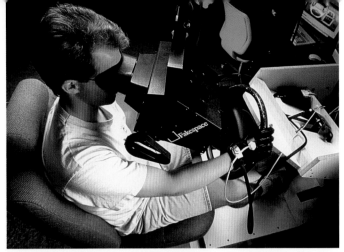

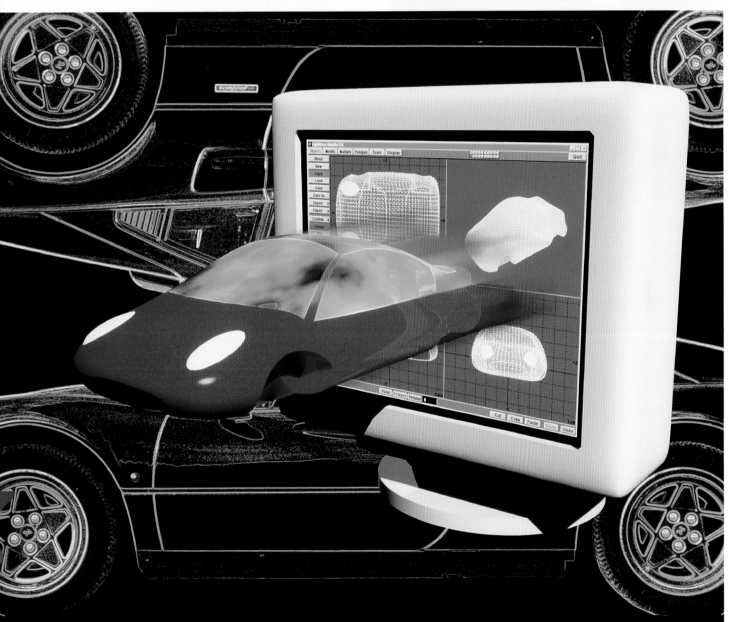

ease of egress they found in taller vehicles, especially in something called a sport utility vehicle. Yet people didn't want to give up the attributes they enjoyed in their low-slung sports cars, so automakers and their designers and engineers responded, and now we have luxurious and high-powered sport utilities. SUVs, Giugiaro notes, "that have the same speed as a Ferrari."

Not only have vehicles grown, but so have the people inside them. Regardless of a car's exterior dimensions, Giugiaro says, interior space must be maintained, or enlarged, because people are getting larger with each generation. Besides, "the need for comfort is increased because we stay behind traffic lights so long, and there are traffic jams and rush hours." One trend Giugiaro sees for concept cars, and for the production cars that they predict, is that interior design will become increasingly more important, and more challenging. "The interior is the most costly part," he explains. "Styling of the interior," with all of its

details and its requirements not just for comfort but for safety and security, for information and entertainment, "costs twice as much."

Yet exterior design cannot be ignored, because "the interior must be in proportion to what the outside gives you," and, Giugiaro adds, "the first reason why you chose a car is the exterior." Many factors influence a vehicle's shape, and those factors seem to be multiplying. "The world is changing. Cars are changing, and drastically over the next 10 to 20 years," says Ken Okuyama, chairman of the transportation design department at the prestigious and influential Art Center College of Design in Pasadena. Okuyama is a Japanese-born, California-educated designer who spent part of his career in Europe, at Porsche and Pininfarina, where his credits include the Ferrari Rossa concept and Enzo Ferrari production supercar. "When we talk about car design, we tend to think only about exterior styling," he adds. "But design

is much deeper. It's almost like product planning. You need good research and good concepts and good vehicle architecture. The designer doesn't have to be a professional engineer, but you need the skills to talk to them, to the radiator supplier and the bumper supplier. You have to consider the dimensions and proportions, the packaging of the suspension and how you fit the people. After that, you finally get to the styling part of car design, the surfacing and character lines, the headlamps and details."

And, he adds, many of the usual assumptions no longer may apply in a world where instead of those three or four lines of so-called mainstream vehicles, "nowadays we don't have mainstream cars, but a whole bunch of niche vehicles." As a result, he says, instead of automatic facelifts every few years, the auto industry should ask itself if society really needs this vehicle, or even this brand, or if there is a better way to fill societal needs.

"I would love to see how the public and people in different cultures would react to radically different ideas of concepts and transportation," says Brigid O'Kane, who moved from designing cars and concepts for General Motors to teach tomorrow's designers at the college of design, architecture, art and planning at the University of Cincinnati. "The width of vehicles was created by the width of the ruts made by [horse-drawn] buggies and it really hasn't deviated," she notes. "There are so many different options that aren't even explored."

O'Kane is encouraged by the publicity accorded the Segway HT, a Human Transporter developed by medical equipment inventor Dean Kamen. Segway is about two feet wide and rides on two wheels, which are powered by electric motors and are separated by a platform that contains computer controls that keep Segway balanced. Segway's rider makes turns by using a stalk that rises from the platform. Segway can carry its driver and up to 75 pounds of cargo at speeds of as fast as 20 miles per hour for a range of up to 15 miles. "Segway is brilliant," says O'Kane. "It's a different kind of animal, but it's serving the public. It's taking a completely different approach. It's an answer to a problem."

She and her students are working on answers of their own. "We're doing an alternative fuel vehicle. We're pushing the boundaries. I'd don't know what it takes to make the transformation in what we think transportation is, but I would like to see something new.

"There's a responsibility that we have, this generation and our watch on this planet."

So, how does the concept car fit into this much more conceptual side of automotive design? On the theoretical side, former Nissan designer Jerry Hirshberg says: "The trick is to do genuine concept cars, cars that really make you stop and scratch your head, cars like the Ford [electric-powered] Think cars. They're not on the macho extreme, but they are genuine explorations that make you think about getting from point A to point B. And they're kind of risky. While not loving these cars, I give them high marks for being genuine concepts. They were three-dimensional question marks on wheels, not just titillating sexmobiles that don't serve any function.

At the show, everybody was asking the person next to them, 'what do you think?'

For a more practical application, educator Ken Okuyama: "There are two major jobs that concept cars can do. One is to present to the public what could be a production car, what they might be able to buy. Another is to test the public's taste, to present a certain message and to see if the public accepts it. You can do a consumer clinic with pictures [of proposed vehicles], but people may not understand. But when they look at a concept car, they understand right away, and you probably want to test the waters before you invest millions of dollars to build a whole assembly line."

There is a third function that concept cars can provide, Okuyama adds, and that is the role of educational tool. If an automaker plans a radical change in styling, or in powertrain, say switching from an internal combustion engine to fuel-cell power, concept

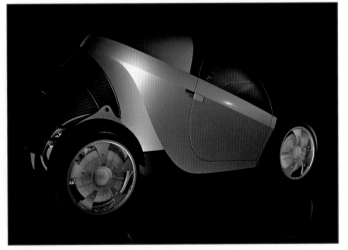

cars can cushion the shock effect by alerting the car-buying public that such a change is coming.

Concept cars also can be used to educate government regulators to new technologies that may need legislative action. For example, cars are required to have a mechanical link between the driver's steering wheel and the steering gear that actually turns the vehicle's wheels. That link is the steering column. But with advances in steer-by-wire technology, a steering column not only is unnecessary, it becomes nothing more than a significant danger to the driver in the event of a frontal collision. Drive-by-wire concept cars such as the Bertone-SKF FILO and Novanta and General Motors' Hy-Wire can show regulators the potential benefits for by-wire drive systems. At the same time, they present designers with many new options for interior styling.

Okuyama offers another example: windshields. "A windshield by law is supposed to be glass," Okuyama says. "Normally," he explains, "the curvature is so little that the difference is little more than half an inch." It needs to be nearly flat to avoid possible distortion of what a driver can see.

Yet glass is heavy, and its naturally flat nature restricts the sculptural shapes that designers can employ. But, Okuyama notes, "the polycarbonate they use in jet fighters is lighter and lasts longer and can be made in any shape. We can experiment with show cars to show the government and public what might be done."

New technologies — whether involving environmentally friendly fuels, new safety equipment (for example, external airbags to protect pedestrians and cyclists) or new windshield materials — bring new design options and challenges. So does designing vehicles for entirely new markets, such as those emerging in nations such as China and India.

"Within 15 years, China will be the major market in terms of production and registration of cars. It's the only market which keeps developing at an exponential rate," says Paolo Caccamo of I.DE.A., an Italian design and engineering consulting firm. "Helping to develop vehicles for Indian and Chinese companies obliges us to keep a very good eye on economy, forgetting perhaps about appearance and 'games' [infotainment], but looking at basic things: safety, handling, powertrain, these sort of things."

Meanwhile, these developing automotive nations are likely to follow a familiar pattern: working with established automakers or consultants and their designers while sending students overseas to be educated in the art and methods of design. At first, design will be tuned to local tastes, but then it will be modified to make vehicles more appealing for export.

But globalization can dilute national style. Remember when you could identify a vehicle's nationality without seeing its badges? For example, and in over-simplified terms, American cars had their

YOUR CAR,

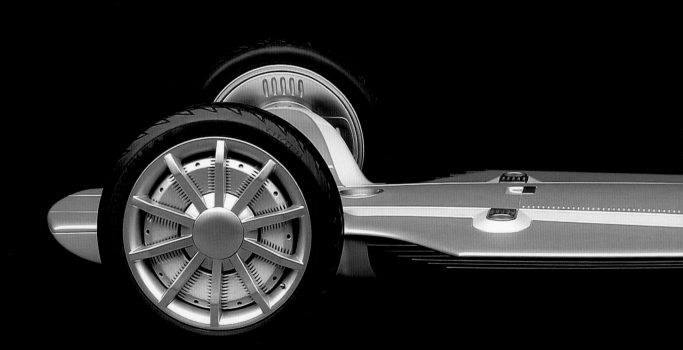

chrome, German cars their efficiency, Italian cars their sensuous lines and French cars their quirks. Export and the spread of similar safety and pollution regulations led to cookie-cutter cars, bean-shaped coupes and sedans and boxy SUVs. But in the early years of the new millennium there is momentum to re-establish not only corporate styling themes but national design identifies.

"It is important to maintain cultural identities," says Patrick Le Quement of Renault, who offers some only slightly tongue-in-cheek examples: the Italians, he says, develop a shape that is visually pleasing, then eventually get around to trying to fit people into that shape. On the other hand, the French, he says, a so obsessed with intelligence and conceptualization that they design cars from the inside out. Like their country, Americans do everything on a larger scale and then step back to enjoy the view, but in the process often overlook the fine and important details.

Meanwhile, there isn't room to step back for such a view in Japan, so Japanese design becomes a fascinating gathering of details, very good details that invite close reading, he adds.

"There have been times when design influences and the focus on design have been high and there are periods when it's been lower, but design has always been the differentiator," adds Wayne Cherry, vice president of design for General Motors. Like design itself, concept cars go through cycles, from blue-sky, designer dream machines to those that are thinly disguised versions of vehicles about to go into series production, and back to again.

"Show cars are starting to push the limits again," says Dragan Vukadinovic, a native of Yugoslavia who grew up in the Midwestern heartland of the United States, studied design in California and worked for Mitsubishi before becoming senior designer at South Korean automaker Hyundai's California studio.

"Originally, they were totally impractical," Vukadinovic notes. "Then Chrysler was the moving forced behind making show cars a preview of production cars, and a lot of car companies fell in behind that kind of thinking." But Vukadinovic says the radically impractical concept cars shown at Tokyo have challenged other design departments to become more free thinking, to bring fantasy back into their concepts.

"It's about getting emotion back into design," says Lincoln Mercury design director Gerry McGovern. "I honestly believe that people, when they look at something they desire, it's not about the fact that it's technically incredibly innovative. Technology has become a given. When people look at cars, they sometimes don't know what it is that spins their wheels, but I believe it's the emotion, and the way we feel when we drive."

And isn't that the point of concept cars: to drive us wild!

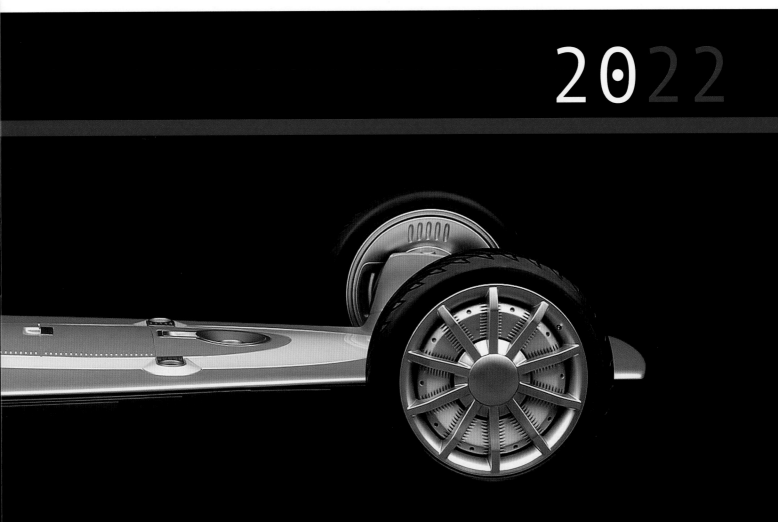

2022

BIBLIOGRAPHY

Books

A Century of Car Design, Penny Sparke, Barron's Educational Services, Hauppauge, New York, USA, 2002

A History of the New York International Auto Show, 1900-200, Greg D. Merksamer, Lionheart Books, Atlanta, Georgia, USA, 2000

American Dream Cars: 60 Years of the best concept vehicles, Michel J. Frumkin and Phil Hall, Krause Publications, Iola, Wisconsin, USA, 2002

Auto 2010: The Car Magazine from the Future, Paul VanValkenburgh, Published by the author, Seal Beach, California, USA, 1991

Car-Men 5: Giorgetto Giugiaro & Fabrizio: Italdesign, Giuliano Molineri, Automobilia s.r.l, Milan, Italy, 1999

Car-Men 7: Franco Mantegazza & I.DE.A Institute, Enrico Leonardo Fagone, Automobilia s.r.l., Milan, Italy, 2000

Cars Detroit Never Built: Fifty Years of American Experimental Cars, Edward Janicki, Sterling Publishing, Main Street Book, New York, New York, 1990

Cars Europe Never Built: Fifty Years of Experimental Cars, Gregory Janicki, Sterling Publishing, New York, New York, 1992

Cars That Never Were, Consumer Guide, Publications International, Lincolnwood, Illinois, USA, 1994

Concept Cars: An A-Z guide to the world's most fabulous futuristic cars, Chris Rees, Anness Publishing, London, UK, 1999

Detroit Dream Cars, John Heilig, MBI Publishing, St. Paul, Minnesota, USA, 2001

Dream Cars: Style for Tomorrow, Serge Bellu and Peter Vann, Motorbooks International, Osceola, Wisconsin, USA, 1989

Ferrari: Design of a legend, the official history and catalog, Gianni Rogliatti, Sergio Pininfarina and Valerio Moretti, Abbeville Press, New York, New York, USA, 1990

Highways to Heaven: The AUTO Biography of America, Christopher Finch, Harper Collins Publishers, New York, New York, USA, 1992

Italdesign: Thirty Years on the Road, Luca Ciferri, Italdesign, Moncalieri, Italy, 1998

Modern Chrysler Concept Cars: The designs that saved the company, Matt DeLorenzo, MBI Publishing, Osceola, Wisconsin, USA, 2000

Pace Cars of the Indy 500, L. Spencer Riggs, Speed Age Publisher, Fort Lauderdale, Florida, USA, 1989

Retrofuturism: The car design of J Mays, The Museum of Contemporary Art, Los Angeles, Universe Publishing, Rizzoli International Publications, New York, New York, USA, 2002

Standard Catalog of American Cars, Standard Catalog of Imported Cars (various volumes), Krause Publication, Iola, Wisconsin, USA

The Art of American Car Design: The Profession and Personalities, C.Edson Armi, The Pennsylvania State University Press, University Park, Pennsylvania, USA 1988

The Car Design Yearbook 1, Stephen Newbury, Merrell, London, UK, 2002

The Creative Priority: Driving innovative business in the real world, Jerry Hirshberg, HarperBusiness, New York, New York, USA, 1998

The GM Motorama: Dream Cars of the Fifties, Bruce Berghoff, Motorbooks International, Osceola, Wisconsin, USA, 1995

Twenty Years of Giugiaro Design, Giugiaro Design spa, Turin, Italy, 2001

Additional publications

Automakers concept car media guides, Various international auto shows

Cadillac & Pininfarina: An Enduring Relationship, Cadillac Communications, Detroit, Michigan, USA, 1999

Christie's Dearborn auction catalog, Dearborn, Michigan, USA, 2002

Detroit News, Detroit, Michigan, USA

Il Museo dell'Automobile (guidebook to the collection of The Automobile Museum), Priuli & Verlucca, Turin, Italy, 2002

Russo and Steele auction brochure, Monterey, California, USA, 2002

Magazines

Auto & Design, Turin, Italy

AutoWeek, Detriot, Michigan, USA

CAR, London, England, UK

Intersection, London, England, UK

Metropolis: Architecture, Culture, Design, New York, New York, USA

Popular Science, New York, New York, USA

Road & Track, Newport Beach, California, USA

AKNOWLEDGEMENTS

The author is grateful for the time that more than 30 automotive designers, working and retired, as well the concept car builders, collectors, design instructors and others provided him with their openness, honesty and patience in answering his questions. He also is indebted to those who helped set up those interviews, especially to Lisa Barrow, Dean Case, Luca Ciferri, Cerys Jones, Sam Locricchio and Wendi Parson for their amazing cheerfulness in the face of his frequent and sometimes frantic calls for help.

The author also must acknowledge the fact that he received this assignment only because his friend and colleague Matt DeLorenzo was too busy to write the book himself, so he recommended me to White Star Publishers.

My hope is that this book informs and entertains, and also advances at least slightly the literature of concept cars and automotive design.

Finally, this book is dedicated with gratitude to three men who left us without knowing the depth of the influence they had on the design of my life: a grandfather who showed me the wonder of words, a father who showed me the wonder of the world, and a mentor who showed me how the automobile could bring those words and that world together.

Larry Edsall

The Publisher would like to thank:
Francesco Pagni, Anna Artigiani – Pininfarina Spa
Franco Bay – Italdesign-Giugiaro Spa
Cerys Jones – I.DE.A. Institute
Germana Martino – Fioravanti Srl
Janis Little – Mitsubishi Motors North America
Jose Paris – Ford Motor Company
Malcom Welford – Christie's International Motor Cars
Michelle Katz – Art Center College of Design, Pasadena

PHOTOGRAPHIC CREDITS

Page 1 Prisma Design International
Pages 2-3 Peter Vann
Pages 4-5 Autogerma spa
Page 7 Fotostudio Zumbrunn
Page 8 center Art Center College of Design
Pages 8-9 Autogerma spa
Pages 10-11 Art Center College of Design
Pages 12-13 Michael Furman Photography
Pages 14-15 center General Motors Company
Page 14 bottom General Motors Company
Page 15 top General Motors Company
Page 15 bottom General Motors Media Archives
Page 16 top National Automotive History Collection
Page 16 center National Automotive History Collection
Page 16 bottom National Automotive History Collection
Pages 16-17 Hulton Archive/Archivio Laura Ronchi
Page 18 top Bettmann/Corbis/Contrasto
Pages 18-19 Michael Furman Photography
Page 19 top Peter Vann/Automedia
Pages 20-21 Michael Furman Photography

Page 20 center Henry Ford Museum
Page 20 bottom Henry Ford Museum
Page 21 bottom right Bettmann/Corbis/Contrasto
Page 22 top left Peter Vann/Automedia
Pages 22-23 Peter Vann/Automedia
Page 22 center Peter Vann/Automedia
Page 23 top Peter Vann/Automedia
Pages 24-25 Michael Furman Photography
Page 24 bottom Rykoff Collection/Corbis/Contrasto
Page 25 bottom John Lamm
Page 26 top Henry Ford Museum
Pages 26-27 Henry Ford Museum
Page 27 bottom National Automotive History Collection
Pages 28-29 Ron Kimball Photography
Pag 28 bottom Bettmann/Corbis/Contrasto
Page 29 bottom Ron Kimball Photography
Page 30 top left Underwood Photo Archives
Page 30 top right General Motors Company
Pages 30-31 Bettmann/Corbis/Contrasto
Page 31 top right General Motors Company

Page 31 bottom right Bettmann/Corbis/Contrasto
Page 31 bottom left Underwood Photo Archives
Page 32 top Bettmann/Corbis/Contrasto
Page 32 bottom Henry Ford Museum
Page 33 top Hulton Archive/Archivio Laura Ronchi
Pag 33 bottom Henry Ford Museum
Pag 34 top TRH Archives
Pag 34 bottom Hulton Archive/Archivio Laura Ronchi
Page 35 top Giles Chapman Library
Pag 35 bottom left Hulton Archive/Archivio Laura Ronchi
Page 35 bottom right Bettmann/Corbis/Contrasto
Page 36 top Henry Ford Museum
Pages 36-37 Peter Vann
Page 36 bottom Henry Ford Museum
Page 37 top Henry Ford Museum
Page 37 bottom General Motors Media Archives
Page 38 top right Archivio Storico Pininfarina
Page 38 bottom Hulton Archive/Archivio Laura Ronchi
Page 39 center Hulton Archive/Archivio Laura Ronchi
Page 39 bottom Giles Chapman Library

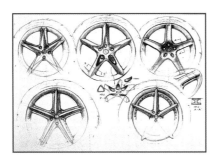

220 Pininfarina's Rossa concept for 2000 celebrated both the Italian design house's 70th anniversary and its long relationship with Ferrari. Detailed drawings of the wheel design provide only a hint of the work involved in making myriad parts into a cohesive concept. While a thoroughly modern vehicle, the Rossa pays homage to classic Pininfarina and Ferrari design elements, interpreted and pushed forward for the new millennium. An example is the way the top of the engine bulges through the hood, reminding tifosi of the 1958 Testa Rossa's protruding carburetor intake stacks.